My Body
GOD'S
TEMPLE

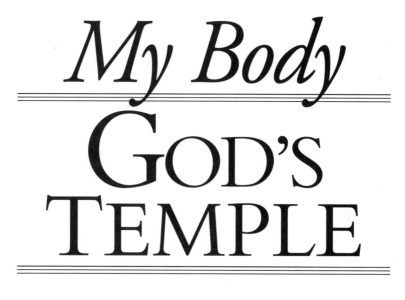

My Body
GOD'S TEMPLE

Joseph Christiano, ND, CNC

A STRANG COMPANY

My Body, God's Temple by Joseph Christiano, ND, CNC

Published by Siloam

A Strang Company
600 Rinehart Road
Lake Mary, Florida 32746
www.siloam.com

Unless otherwise noted, all Scripture quotations are from the King James Version of the Bible.

Scripture quotations marked NAS are from the New American Standard Bible. Copyright © 1960, 1962, 1963, 1968, 1971, 1972, 1973, 1975, 1977 by the Lockman Foundation. Used by permission. (www.Lockman.org)

Cover design by Judith McKittrick
Interior design by Terry Clifton

Library of Congress Cataloging-in-Publication Data

Christiano, Joseph.

My body-- God's temple / Joe Christiano.

p. cm.

Originally published: Orlando, Fla.: Trinity Pub. & Marketing Group, c1997.
Includes bibliographical references.

ISBN 1-59185-415-6 (pbk.)

1. Physical fitness--Religious aspects--Christianity. 2. Christian life. I. Title.

BV4598.C47 2004

248.8'8--dc21

2004002475

This book is not intended to provide medical advice or to take the place of medical advice and treatment from your personal physician. Readers are advised to consult their own doctors or other qualified health professionals regarding the treatment of their medical problems. Neither the publisher nor the author takes any responsibility for any possible consequences from any treatment, action, or application of medicine, supplement, herb, or preparation to any person reading or following the information in this book. If readers are taking prescription medications, they should consult with their physicians and not take themselves off of medicines to start supplementation without the proper supervision of a physician.

04 05 06 07 08 — 987654321
Printed in the United States of America

DEDICATION

In 1979 I was a competitive power lifter and bodybuilder. During that time, a question posed to me by a messenger of God changed the destiny of my life. His question not only was the seed that changed the direction of my life but also in part has now burst forth in the writing of this book. His question to me was direct: "Are you using that body for Jesus?"

It wasn't but a few years later that I met that Jesus who became the Savior of my soul, and from that moment on, the seed has been growing.

A short few years after my spiritual experience, I met Lori, who eventually became my wife. Since then our journey together has been anything but smooth sailing. But we came through every physical, emotional, and spiritual issue we faced with flying colors. Our marriage has been a matter of teamwork with both of us benefiting from the other's strengths. And the glue that keeps this teamwork intact is the Savior of our souls—Christ Jesus.

As I have learned to appreciate His gift to me, I realize how I have been able to do more and accomplish more than I could imagine possible. To sum up my gratitude for being there through all our challenges as well as those that came against the writing of this book, I dedicate this book and poem to my wife, Lori.

Lest she be a loving wife a man would not be
whole,
Lest she be a godly wife a man would have an
empty soul.
Lest she be a supportive wife his potential he'd
never know,
Lest she be a faithful wife his life and purpose
would slowly go.
Lest he realize who she is he could never
accomplish his dream,
But only then is God's gift to him the source
for making a successful team.

ACKNOWLEDGMENTS

When it comes to the writing and editing of a book there is never one single person who can get all the credit. It really takes teamwork to turn a concept into a finished product. I want to thank Barbara Dycus (my ray of sunlight) for meeting all my requests and overseeing the entire project; Jevon O. Bolden for her fine-tuning talents; and Deborah Moss for her proofing of this work.

For her in-depth theological background and a heartbeat that lined up with mine for this work, I thank Carol Noe.

I also want to thank the graphic design and marketing teams for their unique and talented contributions.

Finally, I thank my Creator God for His absolute perfection, unconditional love, and anointing for this work.

CONTENTS

Contents

INTRODUCTION

"**A**nd the house which I am about to build will be great; for greater is our God than all the gods" (2 Chron. 2:5, NAS). King Solomon's statement not only demonstrated the wisdom and perspective that was required for building an awesome temple, but it also exposed his vision for his destiny and purpose, which was driven by his primary motive—love.

By virtue of inheritance Solomon assumed the throne of Israel from King David his father. The responsibility that was placed upon Solomon to rule such a great people was enormous, something far beyond description. This awesome kingdom established and ruled by King David for forty years was the greatest among all the other kingdoms of the world. In addition to the overwhelming demands and responsibilities that came with this leadership position, not to mention the accountability to God, we find Solomon four years later on the threshold of facing another extraordinary task—the building of the temple.

This book is about building a body for victory and, for comparison, shows the unlimited commitment that King Solomon was willing to pour into the building of the temple. The comparison of Solomon's temple and your physical body is so profound and insightful that you will be inspired and encouraged to become your own builder of a body built for victory, destiny, and purpose.

As you know, the temple was a dwelling place for the presence of God and the ark of the covenant, which was placed behind the veil. As you read this book, you will see the wonderful parallels between the temple that Solomon built and your physical body. You will no longer limit your expectations to just the physical rewards associated with taking care of your body. A body built for victory is more than just biceps and waistlines. It includes all of you: body, soul, and spirit, God's original design for humankind. As you understand the connection between a healthy body, a positive mind, and spiritual motivation involved in your total being, you will see beyond the physical and will begin to experience a deeper expression of worship. The reality of walking in victory, purpose, and destiny will overwhelm you as you discover that this whole physical fitness thing isn't about you after all, but rather about God and your love for Him.

My motive for writing this book, besides providing you with all the "tools" and "floor plans" necessary for building your body, is to open your spiritual eyes so you can experience a deeper, richer, and more meaningful reason to be faithful with your physical body. Just as the majesty of Solomon's temple reached far beyond the Israelite kingdom into the lands of their heathen neighbors, this book will open your mind to a purpose that reaches far beyond the physical blessings of building and maintaining a healthy body.

In natural health and even some sectors of the medical community, we agree that one can enjoy the reality of a healthier, more productive, and more active life by simply including regular exercise, proper diet, dietary supplementation, exposure to sunshine, proper breathing, and positive thinking. These healthy lifestyle principles provide greater benefits than just a means for improving one's aesthetics; they are necessary for long-term body, soul, and spiritual balance. A common attitude for taking care of the body has always been for self-gratification, which causes a person to go to the extreme and become obsessed with his or her body. This motive will leave a void and keep you unfulfilled. This same motive will not only allow me the opportunity to challenge your thinking, but also to encourage a new mind-set that has not been clearly understood until now!

As we look again at the story of Solomon's temple, we see that the project required all the resources he was humanly able and willing to use for his primary purpose, which was to build a "great house" that would be pleasing and acceptable to God. Because Solomon's motive was to bring honor to God and not himself, God filled the house with His presence. As you develop your motive for honoring God with your body, it becomes a temple of honor, and therefore the effort will not be in vain.

There is no getting around it: to improve your health, bodily functions, and appearance you have to include certain healthy lifestyle practices regularly in your life. As your coach, I will help you apply the physical disciplines necessary for a body built for victory and expose you to the emotional and spiritual areas of your life.

Have you been struggling with your weight or your health? Do you lack self-control? Perhaps you are convinced that it's time to start doing something to improve your physical self, but you have been putting it off. If so, I want you to know that there is hope. Maybe you have tried before but failed, or perhaps you have been working at it for some time now but need a deeper purpose to keep you focused. Well, allow me to challenge your thinking with a spiritual perspective for being healthy and fit.

As you take it step by step through the building phases, your new body will not only represent discipline and self-control, but it will also be an inspiration to all.

In phase one you will learn the importance of building

from the inside out. In phase two you will learn why certain foods should be avoided in order to maximize your health. Phase three provides you with suggested nutritional supplementation to boost your bodily functions. Phase four provides several specific exercise plans that can be implemented at home, in the gym, or while traveling. In section three, "Builders in Action," you will follow a twelve-month blueprint to nourish and strengthen your body and soul.

But before you put on your sweats and tennis shoes or start planning out those healthy meals and taking your supplements, keep these four key components in mind.

1. Lordship—your body belongs to God.
2. Stewardship—faithful caretaking of your body is your reasonable service.
3. Motive—your love for God is what motivates you.
4. Dedication—you are committing your bodybuilding effort to God's glory.

WARNING: Don't be shocked when, once you get into shape, someone comes up to compliment you on how good you are looking. For it is His physical blessings that will become the opportunity for introducing them to the One who resides inside!

SECTION ONE

Builder's Motivation

CHAPTER 1
First Things First

"**W**here do I begin? How do I go about getting healthy? Why bother?"

There is so much information on the market today promoting different kinds of fitness programs and exercise machines, telling us what diet plan is the best, which supplements to take, the best exercise program to follow, tips for antiaging, weight loss, increasing energy, and avoiding disease. Overwhelmed, many people admit, "It's driving me crazy!" And, feeling helpless, they conclude, "Why bother?"

Let me help you answer this important question in simple terms. I don't blame you if you are frustrated, because you are right—there *is* a lot of health and fitness information out there that can overload your brain. Realizing that fact, as a nutrition and exercise coach for over thirty years, and more recently as a naturopathic doctor, I decided to approach this whole concept of building a healthier, more energetic body as simply as possible. My goal is to help as many people as I can live a life that's free from unnecessary illness and disease. I hope that in reading this book you will honestly receive the answer to your question "Why bother?" as I impart to you the simple answers I believe God has given me, which have helped many people.

THE BUILDER'S METAPHOR

Since this book is about building a healthy body, I have chosen to use the builder's metaphor from a contractor's perspective. No, I don't have an extensive background in the building industry, nor am I a building contractor. However, the experience my wife and I are having in building our new home has helped to unfold the power of this metaphor, teaching me about the *phases* and *procedures* one must go through in the construction of a home. These processes show remarkable similarities to the processes involved in building a healthy body.

Let me warn you in advance, as my contractor warned me at the beginning of our house-building project: there will be unexpected challenges to face along the way. But if you take it step by step and stay focused on the goal, you will eventually see the task to completion, and you will even appreciate more the health you achieve because of the challenges you conquered to reach your goal.

While I am a novice builder in the area of construction, I do have a very extensive background in building healthy physical bodies. I have overseen successful projects that have been transformed from fat to fit, poor health to good health, tired to energetic, weak to strong, and frumpy to beautiful—so you are in good hands. I have had the opportunity to redesign bodies for those who have won Miss America contests, as well as for Hollywood celebrities and other international stars during the years I traveled extensively as corporate fitness trainer for Planet Hollywood. These opportunities came as a result of gaining national recognition from personally winning body-building championships (first runner-up in the Mr. USA contest) and establishing multiple fitness studios where I helped establish the concept of the "personal" trainer.

So you aren't interested in becoming a bodybuilder, you say. Relax. Those foundational years of my life's vocation gave me a great deal of knowledge and understanding of the whole arena of health and fitness. However, my personal motivation and goals for life in general, and specifically my zeal to help others achieve greater health, are quite different now than they were then. For every person, achieving optimum health is necessary to enjoy the life God created you to enjoy. I am convinced, by my experience, that I can help you to do that. Following the principles, phases, and procedures for building health outlined here will help you reach the goals you desire, as it has for so many others with whom I have shared these simple principles.

> *For every person, achieving optimum health is necessary to enjoy the life God created you to enjoy.*

Building your body for victory, with long-term health and vitality, is similar to building a house because both projects begin with a plan. But before I lay out the building plans for you and show you the phases and tools you will be using, let's establish the basis for any successful plan—the attitude you will need to embrace. Cultivating a proper attitude is the key to successful completion of the project. However, unlike building a home, which can be accomplished in a relatively short time, the attitude required to build good health involves a lifetime of commitment.

CHAPTER 2
Commitment to Success

Most of us know *what* we want to achieve regarding our health, but many do not know *how* to achieve it. So before you put on your hard hat and tool apron, let's talk about the mental side of your building project—the commitment required to succeed. If you are truly concerned about the condition of your body and health, and determined to do something about it, you will realize very soon into the project what a huge role your mental attitude plays in the scheme of things.

WILLINGNESS TO MAKE CHANGES

The first aspect of mental attitude you have to consider for refurbishing, redesigning, strengthening, and making your body healthier is the vital role your personal *willingness* plays in making healthy lifestyle changes. So in the planning stage of building your body for victory over disease, illness, and general deterioration you must ask yourself, "Am I *willing* to make the changes necessary to achieve my goals?"

If you think you can transform your body—expecting a life of endless energy that is full of vitality with less disease and ailments—without making a commitment or exerting any effort, you can forget it! You have to cultivate an attitude that transcends a mere fleeting thought or half-hearted whim to improve your health. Your attitude must involve commitment to success. Otherwise, you shouldn't bother considering a plan at all, because it will only set you up for failure.

You have to be willing to acquire the mental edge required for complete fulfillment of your goal. In order to improve your health, a positive mental attitude is also required to enable you to change your lifestyle for a lifetime. This enthusiastic willingness and determination toward change will ensure your success far more than any expensive protocol, exercise machine, or diet plan ever can.

> *You have to cultivate an attitude that transcends a mere fleeting thought or half-hearted whim to improve your health.*

I have seen many people decide to do something about their health and physical condition. They get all excited for a few days and in their enthusiasm declare that they are willing to do anything it takes. But soon after they plunge into the icy waters of healthy lifestyle changes, they find themselves swimming to the side of the pool, giving up their short-lived pursuit of health. They were not aware that the key ingredient for taking care of their physical bodies is the mental aspect—maintaining willingness, a commitment to success, and a positive attitude toward change.

If you choose to accept what I am saying to you, you can avoid the pitfalls of the quitter and fulfill your goals for a healthy body and positive mind that will last for the long haul. That will require mental discipline and personal commitment. Let me encourage you that the power you need to sustain a positive mental attitude to accomplish your goals is available to you. We will address the Source of that power in this section.

FORGETTING THE PAST

First of all, I want you to look beyond your past experiences, failures, disappointments, and frustrations. We have all suffered ill-fated defeats along the way to reaching our goals for health. Don't let those negatives in your past influence your future. Be willing to think "outside the box" to establish a new pathway for a healthy lifestyle. You must be willing to break away from the "pack" and put the blinders on to keep your personal destiny in plain view. I want you to see yourself as being a pacesetter—not a follower!

At every step, I want you to look beyond each challenge that comes your way to focus on your desired goal. Even the most elaborate blueprints don't accurately reveal the beauty of the building they represent; the plan is not fully comprehended until its completion. So it is with building a healthy body—the benefits and satisfaction cannot all be imagined during the building process. I believe you can achieve anything you will put your mind to if you maintain a *willingness* to do it!

Any negative thought patterns that you have adopted in your psyche, such as an expectation for failure or a lack of faith, can become mental roadblocks that threaten to keep you from reaching your fullest potential. Before you can begin to accomplish your purpose and live out your destiny in life, these negative-thinking patterns must be acknowledged, addressed, and removed. They must be replaced with positive, faith-believing, empowering thoughts that produce a positive attitude. I cannot overemphasize how vitally important your attitude is to the building process; it directly determines the limits you place on yourself that keep you from reaching your fullest potential. A positive attitude can lift you high above every stumbling block and adversity that would interfere with your vision and purpose. So, the first question you must ask yourself is, *Am I willing to change?* Only you can determine the answer to that question.

Your life, as you define it today, can take on a whole new meaning once you open your mind to the wonderful potential that lies beyond your present experience. You can reach that potential by learning how to work effectively with what you have and by maximizing your efforts so you can really enjoy the best that life has to offer. This process is similar to deciding what fixtures, rugs, tiles, cabinets, and other décor you want for your new home; you can only design and build with what you have to work with or can afford.

FOCUSING ON THE POSITIVE

If you can accept the fact that a positive attitude is the key that will unlock your potential, there's a brand-new life just waiting for you to enjoy. As you begin to embrace this positive attitude, it will affect your whole being. You will begin to think more clearly, your thoughts will become more positive, your vision will broaden, and your expectations will be higher. Even what you considered your limitations will become stepping-stones that will liberate you to discover greater potential.

> *Negative thought patterns must be replaced with positive, faith-believing, empowering thoughts that produce a positive attitude.*

Your positive attitude will also have an impact on others in inspirational ways. You will personally experience more confidence and assertiveness. You will look good and feel good about yourself. As you go through the building process, accepting its challenges, you will discover how subtly the positive mental attitude, no longer a challenge, becomes a permanent part of your life. Cultivating your positive mental attitude toward making healthy lifestyle changes is like taking your lofty visions of your dream house and giving them to the architect. At that point, you will see them begin to take on life in the form of the floor plans, then the breaking of ground; eventually, the reality of your new dream house is completed.

Having a body built for victory and living in vitality and optimum health are like acquiring a brand-new life! When I talk about cultivating a positive attitude, I am trying to create the understanding that this building process involves your whole being—including your soul and spirit, not just your physical body. Of course, a healthy lifestyle involves physical changes through exercise, diet, and nutrition. However, developing the proper mental attitude needed to make these changes will have a strong impact on your emotional and spiritual life as well.

As you watch the architect put your dream house into floor plans, you begin feeling more excited and energized as you see an image of your dream house taking its initial form. Likewise, if you can identify the important values of your personal life, the desires that truly motivate you, these will energize you throughout the building phases of achieving a healthy body. Establishing *personal motivation*, after cultivating a positive attitude toward change, is the second phase that will help you succeed in reaching your goals of long-term health.

PERSONAL MOTIVATION

Personal motivation is the solid foundation needed for creating a positive attitude, making it a key to successful, healthy lifestyle changes. We all understand the importance of a solid foundation when it comes to building a house. Its main function is to provide stability and support that will endure for the entire life of the structure being built. In Florida, where I live, a house or building is erected on top of a concrete slab, which is poured right on top of the sandy soil. In contrast, building procedures in northern states often involve laying a foundation by digging a deep hole and pouring a basement floor.

Regardless of what method is used for laying the foundation of a building, it is vital to the strength of the foundation that the correct mixture of materials be used in order to prevent future cracks from developing. Your personal motivation is similar to the concrete foundation or slab of a building, when considering the task of developing a body built for victory. Correct motivation will support your positive mental attitude and carry you not only through the building phase, but also through an entire lifetime of health. It is the "proper mixture" of motives that will determine the strength and endurance of your "building"—the healthy body of your dreams.

Motivation comes in many "shapes" and "sizes," usually stimulated by what you have heard, seen, experienced, and what you think and/or feel. For example, if you notice a positive change in the way a person looks who has lost a lot of weight, you can be motivated to make some personal changes yourself. Some changes are motivated by unforeseen or untimely circumstances, like a change in your health, which forces you into a different lifestyle. Even the more rare "self-motivated" individuals in the world need some outside influence to motivate them toward effective change.

> *Correct motivation will support your positive mental attitude and carry you through an entire lifetime of health.*

In both temporal and eternal matters, the right motives make all the difference in your experiencing success or failure. For example, being motivated by the many benefits that come from living a healthy lifestyle can help you make needed changes regarding what you put into your mouth. Knowing the direct effect food has on your bodily functions, learning about your potential illness profile, and understanding healthy or defective thinking can also motivate you to change. Understanding the positive effects obtained from taking nutritional supplements, including the improvement of your immune system, digestive system, and other bodily systems, can motivate you to change as well. Realizing the direct physical benefits of an exercise program, such as boosting your energy and stamina, stimulating your immune system, and improving your overall appearance and sense of well-being, can further stimulate you to make the effort required. These health principles provide valuable motives for embracing change—sometimes.

Unfortunately, there are many people who, even with this knowledge, deliberately ignore the information and are unwilling to make changes until disaster strikes in an unexpected health crisis, at which time they become motivated to change. What a sad and reckless attitude toward the gift of life. There are others, who, when facing health issues, would rather take medications and continue down the path of least resistance toward destruction instead of being willing to change their minds and make the necessary healthy lifestyle changes that would prevent further damage to their health. And of course, there are some who, regardless of their poor physical, mental, and spiritual health, are not willing to change their attitude for any reason—for those individuals there is no hope!

WHAT MOTIVATES YOU?

Willingness to change, as I have discussed, is a prerequisite to hope for a better life. I have also explained that making the necessary changes for living a healthy life is dependent upon your personal motivation. If you do not firmly establish your motivation to change, you will struggle at some point with the question, "Why bother?"

You may be motivated by other reasons, equally as important as those listed earlier, for becoming willing to make lifestyle changes for a healthier body. However, when we consider taking care of our physical bodies, we are usually motivated by *physical* need and *emotional* desire for change. These motives are vital to the "mix" for making a strong foundation to prevent it from cracking under the pressure of the "house" we build upon it.

There is another vital area of motivation as well that must be a part of the foundation for your healthy body. It is the most profound, often untapped, part of your entire being—your *spiritual* motivation. Not only will the spiritual aspect of life bring to completion the physical and emotional areas of your life, but this spiritual motivation will also revolutionize your thinking about caring for your body.

SPIRITUAL MOTIVATION

In this book you will learn of the many benefits that a healthy lifestyle brings. In fact, the wonderful results you will experience as you begin to implement your plan will help to keep you motivated, because *it's all about you.* Because you have been so wonderfully designed and formed, many physical, mental, and spiritual benefits are awaiting you as you accept the challenge of change. You were designed with all the biological, physiological, and psychological mechanisms to keep you in good health—a body built for victory!

It's all about you!

It is totally awesome the way human design and the environment that was originally designed for us have been intentionally interwoven so that we can enjoy good health and a long life. For example, the body is made up of a larger proportion of water than any other element, and the earth is filled with water that we can use to replenish the body's needs. The soil of the earth was filled with minerals and other nutrients our body needs, which are transferred to us when we eat the vegetables and fruits that are grown in the soil.

Because you have been so wonderfully designed and formed, many physical, mental, and spiritual benefits are awaiting you as you accept the challenge of change.

When you choose to live in a way that will create and maintain good health, you are the one who benefits, because *it's all about you.* So the positive results of your constant practice of taking care of your body become a strong motivation to keep you on track. Yes, there are wonderful rewards for taking responsibility for your health, which are necessary for a long healthy productive life. Yet, these rewards will remain only one-dimensional if they are motivated by totally self-serving reasons. When life is just all about you, the rewards for maintaining health remain in the temporal realm at best.

It's all about God!

To avoid this selfish motivation of the benefits of a healthy lifestyle, I want to help you consider a higher motivation for change so you don't miss out on the more satisfying, eternal dimension of life in answering the question, "Why bother?" When you open your heart and mind to this deeper dimension of your entire being—body, soul, and spirit—you will realize that it is *not* all about you. To the contrary—*it is all about God, your Creator.*

Scripture clearly states the reason for our very existence was designed by Creator God:

> For we are his workmanship, created in Christ
> Jesus unto good works, which God hath before
> ordained that we should walk in them.
>
> —EPHESIANS 2:10

> Thou art worthy, O Lord, to receive glory and
> honour and power: for thou hast created all
> things, and for thy pleasure they are and were
> created.
>
> —REVELATION 4:11

As you accept this biblical understanding that everything in your life is ordained by a loving God, you will discover that the motivation for faithfully caring for your body extends beyond the physical and emotional rewards and becomes a spiritual issue—an act of worship. Perhaps some who have limited their definition of worship to prayer and singing of hymns may be questioning how the faithful caretaking of their bodies can be an act of worship. The problem is obviously their definition of "an act of worship." Worship cannot be limited to one or two kinds of expression.

True worship is directly linked to the spiritual condition of your heart, which expresses its gratitude to a loving God for the gift of life itself. Taking responsibility to care for that life—body, soul, and spirit—becomes an act of worship in showing gratitude for the life God gave to you. The apostle Paul challenged true believers in this regard:

> I urge you therefore, brethren, by the mer-
> cies of God, to present your bodies a living
> and holy sacrifice, acceptable to God, which
> is your spiritual service of worship. And do
> not be conformed to this world, but be trans-
> formed by the renewing of your mind, that you
> may prove what the will of God is, that which is
> good and acceptable and perfect.
>
> —ROMANS 12:1-2, NAS

Of course, the apostle Paul was not referring to a literal human sacrifice but to our choosing to live in a godly way that would be pleasing to God as a "spiritual service of worship" (v.

1). Paul specifically refers to making our bodies an acceptable sacrifice of worship as well as our minds. He goes on to warn us not to be conformed to this world, which relates to ungodly ways of thinking, causing us to misuse the gift of life.

> *True worship is directly linked to the spiritual condition of your heart, which expresses its gratitude to a loving God for the gift of life itself.*

Motivation for taking care of our bodies, whether we call it a labor of love or a response of gratitude for the gift of life, is based on accepting the responsibility that God gives us to manage that gift. Besides the motivation of receiving physical and emotional benefits for building a healthy body and lifestyle, it is important to consider our spiritual motivation also as a vital part of the foundation of our "dream houses." We will need to develop a spiritual foundation of eternal values, based on correct motivation that supersedes other personal motives as we strive to successfully answer the challenge, "Why bother?"

Since everyone has the innate capacity for worship, it is the focus of that worship that is of utmost importance. That focus will have a direct effect on all of life's decisions, whether they involve how to better serve your fellowman, becoming a missionary, building a business, or making healthy lifestyle changes. In the end, you will not be as responsible for the actual results of your decisions as you are for the heart attitude and motivation for those decisions. Was life all about you and your worship focused on yourself? Or did something you were "creating" become the focus of your worship? True worship of God is expressed by a heart that is focused on God: it is an overflow of our love for Him.

MY NEED TO FACE SPIRITUAL REALITIES

I now recognize that as a young man, I "worshiped" the physical prowess of power lifting and bodybuilding. My heroes were the iron men of the Hercules movies. Inspired by my dad, who supported us by moving tons of steel around all day in the "mill" of Bethlehem Steel, where only the strong survived, I soon took up weightlifting as he had done. Dad could do a 110-pound one-arm press, among his other achievements. He would tell us stories of his soldier life during World War II, when he and his buddies would lift weights during their off-duty hours.

By the age of fourteen, I had outgrown the 110-pound barbell set my older brother had and needed more iron. As a freshman in high school, I stood five-feet-eleven, weighed 180 pounds, and could bench-press 300 pounds. Converting this strength into the sports arena, I became starting fullback on our football team, even though I was bigger than some of the linemen. I still remember running over would-be tacklers as if they were practice dummies. I set high school records in the discus and shot put that weren't broken for ten years. Though I loved the excitement of team sports, pumping iron was my first love.

After graduating high school, completing a two-year hitch in the military, getting married, and having three children, I spent several years operating a sanitation company in Buffalo, New York, which I started from scratch. My goal was to grow the business, sell it, and relocate to the sunny south in Florida to operate my own fitness business. That dream came true and brought me a great deal of success, both personally and financially. However, as is often the case with dreams that are "all about me," my life's dream turned into a nightmare.

As my life began to fall apart, my personal motivation for my well-being did also, and I turned to food for comfort. When I finally realized I was out of control, I had ballooned to an alarming 305 pounds and was trapped in an unhealthy emotional state that fueled the weight problem. I was nervous and anxious and would eat even when I wasn't hungry.

It was during this time that I began to address the deeper spiritual issues of life, out of which personal motivations and goals had grown. In His mercy, God helped me to recognize my "idol" of physical fitness, then changed my heart, through repentance, to love and worship Him, the Giver of all of life. Pumping iron is no longer my first love or the primary value of my life. Amazingly, God still allowed me to pursue my life's training in physical fitness as a part of His destiny for my life. Only now I am motivated to help others achieve the health they seek.

> *In His mercy, God helped me to recognize my "idol" of physical fitness, then changed my heart, through repentance, to love and worship Him.*

In sharing this part of my personal story, I hope to impress on you that to make healthy lifestyle changes just so you can reap the many physical benefits for a lifetime is a one-dimensional approach to life. It amounts to being focused on yourself as your place of "worship." Not only does this approach to life hinder your personal success, but it also wreaks havoc with your relationships with God and with people.

I suggest that you ask yourself, "What is the focus of my worship?" Some people are very motivated to make lots of money so they can have things—lots of things! Obviously their focus of worship is materialism. Others are motivated to be in the limelight and get all the attention—their focus of worship is their ego.

You may be asking, "What does worship have to do with getting my body in shape or being motivated to change?" If you are asking that question, it means you are ready to hear the answer! As the adage goes, "When the student is ready, the teacher will appear." As we explore the spiritual issues involved in becoming successfully motivated to make proper choices for physical fitness, you will receive the answer to your question. Worship is a central theme to all of life since we are receivers of the gift of life. In sheer gratitude for that gift, we need to establish a proper spiritual motivation for life. The New Testament goes even farther, characterizing our bodies as "temples of God."

> Or do you not know that your body is a temple
> of the Holy Spirit who is in you, whom you
> have from God...?
> —1 CORINTHIANS 6:19, NAS

I have discovered that the fullest potential for life cannot be reached without proper spiritual motivation. The strongest motivation you can develop for personal success in the area of physical fitness lies in your willingness to address the spiritual realities of glorifying God in your body. Let me share with you some biblical principles that transformed my life from the failure of personal idolatry to the freedom and satisfaction of walking in personal destiny.

CHAPTER 3
Building a Temple

When God rescued me from the destructive forces of selfish ambition, He also revealed my destiny and the calling on my life to encourage His people to take care of their physical bodies. Learning to love God and His Word, I began to be motivated by spiritual principles for life that I had never understood before. For example, in the Old Testament, 2 Chronicles records a wonderful historical event about King Solomon building a temple for God.

Out of his love for God, Solomon's obedience to build a temple demonstrates a beautiful picture of his motivation to honor God with the best he could offer Him. As I read this account, realizing that God's Word declares that our bodies are to be temples of God (2 Cor. 6:16), it was not difficult to apply the spiritual principles involved in Solomon's building a temple to the building of my own "temple." Solomon declared:

> Behold, I am about to build a house for the name of the LORD my God, dedicating it to Him, to burn fragrant incense before Him....And the house which I am about to build will be great; for greater is our God than all the gods.
>
> —2 CHRONICLES 2:4–5, NAS

God had given King Solomon the honor of building a temple for the worship of God, after allowing Solomon's father, King David, to gather materials for this house of God. Much effort and great wealth had already been invested into this mammoth project to build a temple for the presence of God when Solomon began his reign. That is true also for each of us who have been provided for as children by hardworking parents who invested much time, money, and effort in raising us to adulthood. Were it not for that investment, we would not have the opportunity to choose to become a "temple" for the presence of God.

In obedience to God, Solomon initiated the construction of the temple. In the building of our "temples" we must realize the honor we have been given to house the presence of God and determine to make whatever investment necessary to complete the task. We have been given a valuable stewardship over the resources of the human life we possess; it is up to us how we use them.

HELP NEEDED

Not having the ability or expertise to take on such an enormous task himself, King Solomon hired the finest craftsmen and most skilled specialists from several kingdoms to do the work of building the temple.

Masterful extravagance

Solomon sought out the best men in their unique abilities, masteries, and proficiencies in their craft, because nothing less than spectacular would be acceptable for the building of the temple of God. The king allowed the use of only the very best of materials, timbers, precious metals, gems, and stones. There was no price he wouldn't pay or any effort too great to make the temple as beautiful as possible to honor the great God he loved and served.

As we apply this principle of extravagance to the building

of our physical temples, it is not the cultivation of vanity that motivates us to create as beautiful a temple as possible, but it is the opportunity to honor God. However, if we do not have the expertise or ability to do this task ourselves, we must seek out those who are skilled to help us. It brings great satisfaction to me, as a personal fitness coach, to help those who are building temples for God to understand the "plan" and bring it to completion.

Major time involvement

King Solomon's tremendous undertaking to build a temple for God took seven years of continual hard work and commitment of hundreds of craftsmen. But once the building of the temple was completed, God showed His divine approval by coming to dwell there in His glorious presence (2 Chron. 5:14). It is clear that there was a major time involvement required to construct the temple of God.

> *In building our "temples" we must realize the honor we have been given to house the presence of God.*

It is so common today for people to "attempt" to build physical fitness every January, as part of a New Year's resolution, only to fall back into harmful lifestyles in February. I cannot emphasize enough the lifetime commitment required for the building of your physical health—your temple. As you become motivated to build a "house" for God's presence, you will be strengthened to continue the task long after the enthusiasm of a New Year's resolution dwindles.

Of course, unlike Solomon's temple, God does not wait to come to dwell in your temple until your optimal health is completely established. He comes when you first call on Him for help and change, as He did for me. He strengthens you for the task, revealing His will for your life as you seek to worship

Him and make Him the focus of your life. Yet, it is simply a fact that you cannot walk in the freedom and fulfillment of personal destiny God desires to give you without persisting toward your goals of optimal physical health. God's destiny for your life requires that you be able to enjoy life to its fullest capacity, which can only be done as you experience optimal health.

Eternal value?

Some experts estimate that the value of Solomon's temple by today's currency standards would be in the billions and billions of dollars. For some it might seem like a waste of time, materials, and money to build such an extravagant edifice that would eventually deteriorate. After all, even the best materials and craftsmanship, while standing the test of time, would not last forever. Yet, it was not for temporal purposes that the temple was built, but eternal. How could this building project have eternal value to it—or could it?

As I read this fascinating account of the building of Solomon's temple, I could understand why King Solomon was considered the wisest man who ever lived. In the way he appropriated the wisdom of God when he erected this breathtaking "house," he understood his culture and, indeed, the nature of all mankind. He knew that people were drawn to the spectacular, the extraordinary, the magnificent, and the extreme—exactly as we are today. Solomon knew that if he built such a temple for God, people from miles around would be drawn to gaze with admiration and awe at the extravagantly beautiful edifice.

Ultimately, the influence of Solomon's temple in all its beauty and splendor extended far beyond even the kingdom of Israel, honoring the God of Israel among foreign peoples. God demonstrated His approval of the building of this temple by presencing Himself there in such a powerful way that the priests could not even stand up in the temple. The Scriptures declare that "the glory of the LORD filled the house of God" (2 Chron. 5:14, NAS).

It must have been a profound and earthshaking realization that this "house" made of earthly materials had just become the temple, the dwelling place, of the living God, Creator of heaven and earth. God's presence dwelling in that earthly temple gave it eternal value. Solomon understood that the temple of God, through its extraordinary outward beauty, would draw people who did not worship this God to view its beauty. As they came, they would get to meet the One who dwelt there.

God's destiny for your life requires that you be able to enjoy life to its fullest capacity.

This beautiful Old Testament account of Solomon's temple offers a parallel for the born-again man or woman, whose physical body is "the temple of God" (2 Cor. 6:16). This profound spiritual motivation should be all that is needed to answer the question "Why bother?" when considering the challenge to make healthy lifestyle changes.

What if God wanted to use you (His temple) to impress people and give you influence so that they could get to meet the One who resides inside of you? Would you be ready? Have you been a faithful caretaker of His temple? What is your attitude toward being a faithful caretaker of your physical body? How much are you investing in your body, God's temple?

A PASTOR'S TESTIMONY

In June of 2003, my wife and I had started our Fitness and Fellowship classes at Pastor Sam Hinn's church, The Gathering Place in Orlando, Florida. I had met with some of the leaders of the church to find out what their interests were for the class criteria and to work out the details. Associate pastor Don Newman seemed to be very motivated and ready to get the class started. Yet, from my observation, he was well overweight and walking in defeat. I knew what he needed, but I wanted to know why he thought he wanted it—what was motivating him toward physical fitness?

> For the past seventeen years I had really struggled with my weight. I climbed up in weight over time from 210 pounds to 240 pounds. Turning thirty, being a newlywed, and then starting a family, my life had changed, and so did my metabolism. I soon discovered that my level of stress from my career and family life with all its obligations was sending me to the refrigerator. I began coping with life's issues by eating.

> I made a career change in 1987 and became a state trooper. Now with a job that had plenty of overtime hours, I found myself dealing with new stress and new situations that led me to even more overeating. Before I realized it, fourteen years had come and gone—but not my weight. The police agency had a fitness policy and standards for weight, but no specific plan or concept to follow. I ended up trying every diet plan on the market but to no avail.

> Eventually I left the patrol and went into full-time ministry as an associate pastor. I thought, *Now is my time to lose weight. I won't have those double shifts that brought all that stress, and there will be no more free fast food to turn down.* How wrong could I have been? The way I had dealt with stress and celebration earlier was the same way I was dealing with it now. Plus, I faced a new problem: there were no weight standards for an associate pastor, nothing to keep me accountable. Within three years I zoomed up to 290 pounds. You would

have thought the increase in the size of the slacks I wore would have made me realize what was happening with my weight, but it didn't. It was my health that started to get my attention. From being tired at midday, to having bouts of dizziness, to my concern with the disease and illness that many of my friends and family members were experiencing, my attention focused on my health for the first time in my life. These situations made me want to make the changes, but they didn't give me the power to change.

In May of 2003, after many years of prayer and counsel, God gave me the breakthrough I needed in order to see real change come into my life in the area of my weight and health. Losing one friend to diabetes and another to cancer began the process of change. Even though I believe in divine healing, what struck me most was the fact that many of them—if not all—never got healed. I realized that they would not have experienced failing health if they had shown concern about their health in the first place. God started working on my attitude about the choices I was making. Was I seeking His glory in my life, or was I living out my life on my own say-so? Was I willing to see the vision He had for my life?

Shortly after these eye-openers, I attended a seminar with Dr. Joe Christiano called "My Body, God's Temple." Immediately afterward I approached him with the idea of helping our church staff with their physical health and condition. He agreed to meet with my staff of eight individuals for Fitness and Fellowship classes. He taught us how to implement the blood-type-diet concept and about nutrition and exercise. But he also reminded us that the focal point of taking care of our bodies was all about God, not about ourselves. Over the next three months not only did my dizziness and fatigue disappear, but also my weight. By the end of the ninety-day program I had dropped 60 pounds and had a new body. I was able to buy a new suit—the perfect forty-year birthday gift I had been pressing for.

Today my approach and outlook on eating and exercise are different from what I ever imagined they would be. Today I see that what I do with my body, whether good or bad, has everything to do with my love for God. It is not a matter of how much weight I lose or how good I look in my suit, but most importantly, am I being a faithful steward of His temple?

There is no question about it, and this is true about anyone. When individuals change their mental attitude about taking care of their health, which motivates them to make the proper dietary changes and become more physically active, not only do they look and feel better, but also their entire outlook on life changes. That person is able to do more, endure more, and be more productive in every aspect of their life. They are able to fulfill their God-given destiny for life and handle the adversity that life hands them so much easier.

But the rewards don't stop there. As you have seen before, when individuals lose weight and improve their physical appearance, they are very inspirational to others, particularly if they have been in bad shape for quite some time. Their new, healthier, and more attractive appearance has a magnetic force that naturally draws looks, praises, and appreciation. I

call those comments, "God's positive, emotional, and psychological affirmations for taking care of His temple." They are well
deserving and represent much more than just the cosmetics of
outward appearance.

> *God's presence dwelling in Solomon's earthly temple*
> *gave it eternal value.*

When your body makes healthy transitions and goes
through the natural transformation from being fat to becoming fit, you demonstrate tremendous victory over past defeats
in the areas of self-discipline and self-control. You start experiencing what it feels like to walk in victory over destructive
habits like laziness and self-indulgence, and it feels great! Your
new body reflects the reality of a positive attitude, a willingness to make changes, and an appreciation for your life. The
"new you" has become an inspiration to everyone who sees
you and is struggling with health and weight issues. Without
realizing it, you have made believers of those who have failed
in the past and who gave up, feeling that there was no hope.
You have inspired those who have learned to "own" negative
attitudes and taught them to rethink their attitude about their
laziness.

Our Creator made you and me in such a wonderful and
magnificent way that when we choose to walk in health principles, the rewards are abundant and affect us in every area
of our lives. We have mentioned only a few of the natural
blessings that anyone can experience when they start making healthy lifestyle changes, including becoming a healthy
"dwelling place" for the presence of God, enjoying optimal
health, and influencing others to make healthy choices as well
as learning to know God themselves. As wonderful as these
goals are, there is more.

DEDICATION TO THE GLORY OF GOD

Make no mistake about it, when you make a conscious effort to improve your health and get your body in shape, the wonderful results you achieve may "puff" your ego. Maybe from past personal experiences or observations of others, you know that when there is a positive physical change in one's appearance, attitude, or physical condition, the ego can easily get "stroked." The prevailing side effect of that phenomenon, if you are not careful, will be a "swollen head" (pride)—and who wants to be lopsided? This prideful response always happens when the spiritual focus is you.

That is why I am trying to impress upon you the importance of establishing the proper motivation for the building process. Remember that you want to change your self-serving attitude, the attitude that says it's all about you. This selfish motivation is common to everyone because we are naturally inclined to try to please "self" in all of its demands. Only by renouncing your ego's demands and refusing to be self-absorbed, focusing instead on honoring God with your physical body and your entire being, will your "building project" not be in vain.

There is a fine line between building optimal health for your self-gratification and doing it for God's glory. You must choose honestly whom you will serve. Serving your own ego will keep your life on a one-dimensional plane. If you choose to build a temple for the presence of God, you will discover true destiny for your life. You will enjoy the best of both worlds—improved health and a fit body with all the physical blessings that they provide—and, more importantly, eternal purpose in dedicating to God a body that is built for His glory.

What happened when the glory of God filled His temple? We can only imagine the impact that His almighty presence had on the nation of Israel on the day of the dedication of the temple. King Solomon's prayer of dedication is one of the most beautiful prayers recorded in the Scriptures. As he knelt at the altar in the presence of all Israel, he acknowledged that the temple they had built could not contain God, the Creator: "Behold, heaven and the highest heaven cannot contain Thee; how much less this house which I have built" (2 Chron. 6:18, NAS).

> *There is a fine line between building optimal health for your self-gratification and doing it for God's glory.*

In spite of that reality, King Solomon asked God to honor that place of worship with His presence and to hear the prayers of the people who came there to worship. He asked for forgiveness for sins, both personal and national, and that God would keep His promises to His servant David. (See 2 Chronicles 6.) What is of greatest interest to us as we look at the parallel of dedicating this temple and dedicating our own bodies to the Lord is the response of the people when the presence of the Lord filled the temple:

> Now when Solomon had finished praying, fire came down from heaven and consumed the burnt offering and the sacrifices; and the glory of the LORD filled the house. And the priests could not enter into the house of the LORD, because the glory of the LORD filled the LORD's house. And all the sons of Israel, seeing the fire come down and the glory of the LORD upon the house, bowed down on the pavement with their faces to the ground, and they worshiped and gave praise to the LORD, saying, "Truly He is good, truly His lovingkindness is everlasting." Then the king and all the people offered sacrifice before the LORD.
>
> —2 CHRONICLES 7:1–4, NAS

When King Solomon completed the temple project, God fulfilled His promise to dwell in a temple made with hands. Imagine! The presence of the almighty God had taken up residence in that earthly temple—wow! After all the time investment, the extravagant workmanship, and investment of the best materials, King Solomon's task of building a temple for the glory of the Lord was finished. There was only one thing left to do—dedicate it to the Lord. It was after that dedication prayer that God responded, and the literal presence of God filled the temple.

Dedicating your body to the glory of God is the real turning point in the building project of a body built for victory. When you dedicate the entire process to God—the time, the effort, and the cost—your body will become a temple of honor, filled with His presence. This reality is the ultimate answer to the question: "Why bother?" You can have many reasons for wanting to improve your physical appearance and health, and there is nothing wrong with simply making the needed improvements.

As we have discussed, everyone needs to put forth the effort to improve his or her health for the physiological and psychological benefits alone. This natural responsibility for caring for the gift of life reflects a healthy love for oneself that everyone should have. However, when you become motivated to care for your physical body in order to bring glory to God as His temple, you are reaching toward a dimension of life that has eternal value. That is when your focus, attitude, and motivation have shifted from you to God. Then, God Himself will bless you with all physical blessings, giving you the power and strength you need to be a faithful steward of His temple—your body. The eternal value of becoming a dwelling place for God cannot begin to be estimated.

I am convinced that if the church, that is, every born-again believer, would take seriously the importance of maintaining a healthy lifestyle, repenting of the sins of laziness, abuse and neglect, gluttony, lack of self-control, and hypocrisy that they have committed against God's temples (their bodies), God would deliver them. He would heal their bodies and minds and exalt the beauty of His church so that the world would behold the beauty of the "temples of God" and desire to know Him as well.

> *When you dedicate the entire process*
> *to God, your body will become a temple of honor,*
> *filled with His presence.*

The awesome reality that a holy God would choose to live in a body made of flesh, blood, and bones still blows my mind. Yet it is so, for the Scriptures teach that Christ purchased our bodies through His death on the cross:

> For ye are bought with a price: therefore glorify God in your body, and in your spirit, which are God's.
>
> —1 CORINTHIANS 6:20

And again, the apostle Paul declares:

> But we have this treasure in earthen vessels, that the excellency of the power may be of God, and not of us.
>
> —2 CORINTHIANS 4:7

Having laid the foundation of the highest motivation for pursuing physical fitness and health, which is, of course the spiritual goal that is of eternal value, it is now time to evaluate the nitty-gritty of our present course. Honest evaluation is always required before significant change can be effected in any area of life. That is emphatically true for the area of physical fitness, which is so filled with deceptions of our own design. I encourage you to face your personal "excuses" for limiting your potential for health. In facing them, you will expose their lie and be set free to pursue your divine potential for life and health.

CHAPTER 4
Dietary Dilemma

My God-given passion to help people be healthy does not exclude anyone, regardless of gender, race, religion, creed, or nationality. However, my purpose for addressing the question "Why bother?" is to challenge especially those who belong to the "church." I am not referring to a religious organization, but to the entire body of Christ, made up of born-again believers who have accepted Jesus Christ as their Savior. I believe God has chosen me, among others, to be a messenger to all of God's people who have been deceived by the enemy of their souls in the realm of personal physical health and fitness.

Over time, this deception has blinded their eyes so that many are unaware of their God-given responsibility of the stewardship of their physical bodies. This blindness in turn has caused His people to develop a complacent and mediocre attitude toward living a healthy lifestyle. They fail to realize the negative impact their negligence has on people within, as well as outside, the church. In addition to sinning against the temple of God through slothfulness, believers fail to realize that unbelievers look at them (the church) with the perception of being undisciplined hypocrites.

Unfortunately, I have had firsthand experience, because

of the secular arenas of my profession, to hear these critical observations made many times regarding "plump" and sickly Christians. General disregard for caring for the "temple" of God has hurt the witness of the church by not demonstrating a life of self-control and discipline. Even the hilarious jesting among church members about overeating and "pigging out" reveals their blindness to the sin of gluttony. A cursory observation of the poor physical condition of many in church leadership only strengthens the mixed messages that unchurched people are receiving.

> *General disregard for caring for the "temple" of God has hurt the witness of the church by not demonstrating a life of self-control and discipline.*

Have we considered the wonderful truth of divine healing in light of our disregard for faithfully caring for His "temples"—our bodies? What is wrong with this picture? There is a person suffering from obesity and diabetes who asks for prayer for healing and then picks up a dozen doughnuts on the way home from church. In this situation, the physical illness is likely an outward manifestation of a problem with heart attitude; the root of the problem is spiritual. In many similar situations, God's people are being deceived by our enemy, the devil, believing they can live as they want and then receive God's divine healing when the consequences of their slothful lifestyle causes illness. This is a very similar attitude to believing you can blatantly sin and then ask for forgiveness, without paying the consequences for your sin.

I believe the church of Jesus Christ (each individual member of the body of Christ) should consider the faithful caretaking of their body as a spiritual issue first of all. I believe this attitude toward caring for the physical life God gave us demonstrates our love and gratitude to our Savior who has freely given us eternal life. Because the church has been redeemed by Christ's unconditional love, our entire being—body, soul, and spirit— belongs to Him. (See 2 Corinthians 2:19–20.)

Should people who confess no belief in God be the champions of physical fitness and cultivating health? I don't think so. It is for those who have made Christ Lord, thereby becoming a temple for His presence, who should care most for their bodies. So don't you think it follows that you should be willing to become a faithful steward of your body? That means living a self-disciplined, knowledgeable lifestyle that will ensure optimum health. So far, I have addressed only the "church" regarding our responsibility for nurturing our health. It might be enlightening to know that in many world religions, dietary laws play an integral part in their followers' lives.

DIETARY REGULATIONS IN WORLD RELIGIONS

I chose randomly to discuss dietary regulations strictly followed by the faithful in belief systems other than Protestant, evangelical Christianity. My purpose is, by comparison, to help illustrate how important I believe it is for the church, which is not based in "religion" but in a personal relationship with the Savior, to recognize their godly responsibility to be stewards of their bodies. If followers of world religions can dedicate themselves to man-made religion with its dietary laws and rituals, how much greater should our attitude of dedication, as followers of Jesus Christ, be toward caring for His temple? The answer to this question is an important key to correctly responding to: "Why bother?"

The following chart summarizes some of the dietary restraints practiced by faithful followers of other cultures and religions. While I understand that taking care of your body is not limited to dietary practices, it is interesting to note the care taken by devout religious people regarding the use of food, who may not even base their practices on biblical understanding. (See Appendix A for more specific discussion of dietary regulations.)

GENERAL ROLE OF FOOD IN WORLD RELIGIONS

The following purposes determine the role of food in world religions:

1. To communicate with God through thanksgiving or by asking for blessing
2. To demonstrate faith through the acceptance of divine directives concerning diet
3. To develop self-discipline through fasting or other eating restrictions

Dietary restrictions practiced by world religions may include:

1. Foods from which to always abstain
2. Foods to be eaten only on certain occasions
3. A prescribed time of day when eating is allowed
4. Instructions for preparing certain foods
5. Designated times of fasting, abstaining from all food or certain foods[1]

Many world belief systems practice dietary regulations regarding the consumption of meat. For example, a devout Buddhist or Hindu may follow a vegetarian diet, and a Catholic may choose not to eat meat on Fridays but on other days. A Jew may observe the elaborate and stringent kosher system for eating meat, while an Islamic devotee would avoid pork and alcohol and fast daily during the entire holy month of Ramadan. It is believed that one result of the observance of these "food codes" is the strengthening of group identity.[2]

According to anthropologists:

> Every religion provides ways by which humans can try to relate to a supreme being or some

supernatural force. Many of the practices and beliefs of the various religions are attempts to explain those things which humans themselves cannot understand or control. Each religion has evolved certain rituals or customs, which are important to the members of that religion.

The observance of these rituals and customs is believed to be mandatory since they express and reaffirm the various beliefs of the religion.[3]

For more detailed information on dietary laws and rituals of the Jewish culture, Mormonism, Islam, Hinduism, and Buddhism, please refer to Appendix A. These major religious cultures mandate regulations regarding the eating habits of their followers.

Even among the "branches" of Christianity, the most widely spread of the world's religions, there are strong dietary considerations. Historically, Orthodox Christianity is the oldest branch, with the split between the Orthodox Church in Constantinople and the Catholic Church in Rome dating back to 1045. These early and medieval Christians placed significant religious symbolism on food.[4]

Religious symbolism and food

Early penitents were reminded that sin entered the world when Eve ate the forbidden fruit in the Garden of Eden. They also followed Jesus' teaching regarding the ritual of Communion, which came to mean salvation through eating the bread and drinking the cup of Communion.[5]

During the early centuries of Christianity, gluttony was seen as a major form of lust, fasting was regarded as the most painful form of renunciation (it was required by church law to fast on certain days), and eating (partaking of the Communion) was the most basic and literal way of encountering God. Everyone was required to take Communion at least once a year.

Also, the celebrations of their faith involved feast days, centered on specific foods for particular feasts. For example, the celebration of Christmas (the birth of Christ) included roast beef, Yorkshire pudding, fruitcake, and mince pie. Easter, the celebration of the resurrection of Christ, involved feasting with ham, roast lamb, and the pagan addition of "Easter eggs." There was some variation in these feast foods, depending on the family's country of origin.

Fasting and abstinence

Christian believers have always been subject to regulations regarding the abstinence from food, though these regulations have continually evolved throughout the history of the church. For Roman Catholics in past decades, fasting was required every Wednesday and Friday, as well as during other seasons of Advent (before Christmas) and Lent (before Easter). However, fasting did not mean total abstinence from food. Rather, it applied to certain foods such as meat and animal products. Meat was forbidden for American Catholics on Fridays until 1966.[6]

After the Protestant Reformation (led by Martin Luther, John Calvin, and others) in the 1500s, their followers were released from the Jewish food taboos, based on the biblical reference to Peter's vision, when he was commanded: "What God has cleansed no longer consider unholy" (Acts 10:15, NAS). Whether that was meant to be taken literally regarding the eating of food is left to personal interpretation.[7]

While there are considerable diversities among the many Protestant denominations, there is not much emphasis placed on fasting or observance of holy days, except for Christmas and Easter. Where practiced, fasting is voluntary and is used to facilitate prayer and worship. Only a few Protestant denominations, such as the Seventh Day Adventists, have dietary practices integral to faith. Their founder, Mrs. Ellen White, had numerous visions during the late 1800s, some of which involved health and diet. Her emphasis reflected the time of health reform in which she was living.[8]

Seventh Day Adventists today still follow many underlying beliefs regarding health and diet, including the practice of fasting. They believe that sickness is caused by violations of the laws of health. They believe their health is maintained and preserved by eating the right kinds of food, and they also believe in the importance of rest and exercise. In all things, they teach the practice of moderation. Their list of restrictions and prohibitions includes:

1. Discouraging overeating
2. Prohibiting meat consumption (embracing vegetarianism)
3. No use of alcoholic beverages, coffee, tea (drink water only)
4. No highly seasoned condiments
5. No eating between meals
6. No use of tobacco products[9]

While fasting is not a major theme of Protestants, most have historically prohibited the use of alcoholic beverages, even in the ministration of Communion in the church. In this restraint, they explicitly refer to the fact that the body is the temple of God, which must be protected from consequences of overuse of alcohol. However, more recently, "social" drinking has become more acceptable even among Protestant believers and wine is used more often in many of their Communion celebrations.

ACCEPTED CULTURAL RESTRICTIONS

The purpose of this discussion of cultural and religious dietary restrictions is primarily to demonstrate that for many different religious cultures, these restrictions or regulated eating habits are accepted as a cultural or religious law.

Though most of these religious systems would not consider their body to be the "temple of God," as do evangelical Christians, they allow their religion or culture to dictate how they view certain foods and eating habits. How much more should we, who believe in the stewardship of the body in order to bring glory to God, consider what we put into our bodies on a regular basis and how we treat them with regard to proper exercise? Christians, more than any other religious followers, should not condone self-indulgence, with its consequences of poor health and preventable disease.

EVALUATING DIETARY MOTIVATION

If you look more closely at various religious dietary laws and rituals, you might wonder what could motivate people to obey such restrictive laws. (See Appendix A.) It is safe to say that, in order to be considered a devout believer of any religious system, you would need to obey the dietary laws and rituals. So what motivates these adherents to keep such strict rules regarding what they may or may not eat and when they must refrain from eating? Would obedience itself be the motivating factor? The desire for a clean conscience? Fear? The hope of receiving mercy and love from Allah, Buddha, or another deity? Do they have an innate need to obligate themselves to a strict law?

> *We are motivated by love and faith, which calls forth our best effort to please God.*

Whatever the motivation, it is clear that there is no freedom in keeping religious dietary regulations. Religious law demands obedience, and disobedience brings guilt for breaking the law. When a person's belief system has tentacles running deep into his religion's dietary laws and rituals, his personal sense of acceptance is based upon keeping those laws. There is no freedom. A person is either guilty of breaking the law or accepted by keeping the law. All of life becomes a religious requirement to be met.

In contrast, the attitude of followers of Christ is filled with a desire to please Him. We are motivated by love for God, who has shown us the ultimate love through the gift of Christ. We choose to walk in freedom and liberty by faith in the redemptive work of Christ, which sets us free from "religious duty." We are motivated by love and faith, which calls forth our best effort to please God. Without explicit biblical dietary laws and rituals demanded by God for His people to follow, our motivation for making healthy lifestyle changes (dietary changes) is based on our freedom to choose.

Choosing to be a follower of Christ, we should then desire to become the best person we can to enjoy our relationship of love with Him and to fulfill the destiny He has for our lives. Given this freedom to choose, the follower of Christ can experience dietary freedom as well as freedom to make healthy lifestyle changes. When focusing on the greater purpose of fulfilling personal destiny through a worship relationship with Christ, the believer in Christ will walk in liberty and freedom and not be held in bondage to religious dietary laws.

Free to decide

I respect everyone's right to choose to follow their religion's dietary practices. Whether I agree with their religion or being restricted by dietary laws and rituals is not the issue. My intention here is to provide you with the answer to the question I posed earlier: "Why bother?"

To answer this question we must revisit the discussion of your focus of worship. When your focus of worship is based on your love for God, and not yourself, that love begins to drive your actions, causing you to make healthy choices in every area of life. As we have seen, your entire life—body, soul, and spirit—is about God and His love for you. When you embrace that understanding, you will be filled with desire to set your personal standards higher than others, focusing your worship on God and desiring to fulfill His destiny for your life.

The Bible teaches that when we accept Christ as Savior and Lord we are born again, that is, our spirits are made alive in a relationship with God, and we are given the gift of eternal life. Followers of Jesus Christ know that there is nothing they did or could do to make it possible for them to one day spend eternity in heaven with their Father—God. It is purely by the grace of God and His unconditional love that make that wonderful reality possible.

Mature motivation

The entire life of the born-again Christian revolves around a purposeful pursuit to learn more about God through cultivating a personal relationship with Christ. In doing so we begin to understand the character of God and His great love for us. As we feel His caring and acceptance, we are motivated to increased love, faith, and dependency toward Him. This is what the Bible means when it says, "We love him, because he first loved us" (1 John 4:19).

As we grow in this supernatural relationship, our desire to please Him grows as well. The life of the born-again Christian is not about perfection, performance, or religious ritual. It is all about our relationship with God and how much we love Him. Without the yoke of "legalism," born-again men and women can freely serve God with all their heart, mind, soul, and body. Their "good works" are not works produced by their own power. They are produced by the power of the Spirit of God who resides in them. This is always evident when God is the focus of our worship.

Our walk of faith promotes spiritual maturity in Christ,

which enlightens us to the reality that God is Lord of all things. That means He is the owner of all of our possessions and has given them to us to manage. With that responsibility come the need for accountability and the element of reward. But we are no longer motivated by fear of being guilty of breaking the law. We are humbled by love and a desire to serve our God.

> *Being faithful stewards over the gracious gifts of God should be our main concern as born-again Christians.*

The reality of being a child of the King of kings and filled with the blessed hope of spending all eternity with our God liberates us and sets us free to offer Him our best. This freedom to serve God with an open heart and willing spirit causes excitement and energy in our souls. It is sometimes referred to as the joy of the Lord. Owning the attitude to freely manage everything that God has given us has to be motivated by our love for God. It is the answer to "Why bother?" Being faithful stewards over the gracious gifts of God should be our main concern as born-again Christians.

Pulpits, leaders, and mixed signals

Many believers who desire to please God with their lives include just about every area of their lives—actions, thoughts, attitude, prayer, meditation on the Holy Scriptures, and faithfully serving in their calling. Unfortunately, when it comes to taking care of their physical bodies and health, there appears to be somewhat of a void in this part of Christian practice or living. What happens with their belief system in this area? Although they appear to be motivated to serve God out of gratitude and love for Him, they seem unconcerned, unconvinced, or unaware of their obligation for taking care of God's temple. Does their belief system go into default?

Who is to blame for this common attitude problem in the church? None of us are exempt from weak moments or times of temptation. All of us at one time or another have succumbed to the lusts of the flesh, so who is to blame? Why are most Christian men and women not concerned with their health and bodies? Should the blame be placed on the leaders or the individual Christian, or should the blame be shared?

Let me start at the top with those in leadership positions, because what "monkey sees, monkey does." I want to address the leaders—preachers, teachers, associate pastors, or any leader in any capacity. Those standards that are held by those at the top will trickle down through the ranks and affect those under the authority of that leadership.

More accountability is placed on those who hold a leadership position than upon those who are being led. The Scriptures say, "For unto whomsoever much is given, of him shall be much required: and to whom men have committed much, of him they will ask the more" (Luke 12:48). Leadership in any capacity demands a higher standard of practice—it goes with the territory. Leaders carry a higher level of accountability because they set the pace by the examples their lives give to those under their leadership. Every part of their lives is carefully scrutinized. They have an immense impact and influence upon the people they lead. Leadership does not exempt them from practicing what they preach. It holds them more tightly to a higher standard of practice.

I grew up in a time when kids heard adults say things like, "Don't do as I do, but do as I say." With a parental or authoritative code like that being imposed on kids, it is easy to understand why youngsters get confused and eventually become rebellious.

I firmly believe that God's people have a responsibility for taking care of their physical conditions. But I am also very sensitive to the struggles they face, which ultimately lead to walking in defeat. That is why I feel the need to address these issues by starting with the leaders. The health benefits that accompany a healthy lifestyle should be motivation enough for a leader to model good health practices. I often wonder if leaders are aware of how much preaching they are doing—not by words, but by the actions and practices by which they live their lives.

Throughout my life I have heard many sermons on stewardship. In most cases, money seemed to be the main focus of stewardship. God is clear on the subject of stewardship—He is the owner of all things. As Christians, we are placed in managerial positions and given the privilege of managing what God entrusts to our hands, whether it be money, time, talents, gifts, relationships, ministries—oh, and yes, our physical bodies. Most, if not nearly all, of the sermons I have heard on stewardship did not include the need for us to be faithful caretakers of our bodies—God's temples.

Yes, I have heard, and probably you have too, about the evils of smoking, alcohol, drugs, going to questionable places, keeping company with questionable people, the perils of pornographic materials, and the like. But when was the last time (or first time) that you heard a preacher speak about the evils of overeating, unhealthy eating, gluttony, or being lazy and not exercising the body?

Your physical body is a walking billboard that advertises your act of stewardship.

If you are a leader and are reading this, please know that what I am saying is not meant to condemn or judge you, but instead to make you aware and encourage you to pursue a balance in your life. Your ministerial demands are awesome and, many times, overwhelming, and you have little time for yourself. But this is so for many of us as well. Nevertheless, your role as a leader requires you to consider your lifestyle as well as the content of your message, which includes making a practice of doing the necessary things to keep your body and physical condition healthy. It's not just about your appearance, which does say a lot about your attitude concerning your physical self, but also for long-term fitness and health to better enable you to endure the duties of your calling. Your ministry is all about God, not you. He called you; therefore, it is your responsibility to do all you can to manage and protect your body, mind, and spirit by doing the things you ought to be doing to safeguard it.

Your physical body is a walking billboard that advertises to your congregation and others your act of stewardship. Don't send out mixed signals. I encourage and challenge you to walk the talk. I promise you that, once you make healthy lifestyle practices a part of your life, your body will take on those physical blessings of weight loss, more energy, better sleep, and clearer thinking. You will be free to preach on faithful stewardship of your body and to encourage your listeners with conviction because of your experience and new walk! Run with it—you are the leader!

Who else is there to blame? It's now time to look at ourselves individually. I happen to be the kind of guy who believes that each one of us is accountable for our own actions, thoughts, motives, what we say, how we say things, and so on. I also believe that God holds each of us accountable. I believe in walking the talk, not in absolute perfection, but at least with a conscious effort, attitude, and conviction for maintaining a walk that aligns itself with what one believes. If we are to believe in what the Holy Scriptures tell us regarding our bodies being temples of the Holy Spirit, then why shouldn't each of us take special care, raise the bar of self-discipline, and willingly be faithful caretakers of our physical bodies? The very fact that God has chosen to reside in our earthly bodies should shock us into reality and prompt us to be faithful stewards.

Your walk should line up with your talk and with what you believe. Otherwise, those with whom you come into contact will get mixed signals.

The time has come for God's people to raise the bar, set the pace, and demonstrate before the world, by example, our appreciation and gratitude toward the God we claim to love. He has given us both physical and eternal life.

Since the Scriptures clearly state that our bodies are temples of God and that His Spirit dwells within us, how much more motivation do we need to get off the couch, put down the garbage, and renovate our bodies? Remember that they are God's temples.

A wake-up call

A few years ago, I was invited to conduct a health and fitness seminar at a church up north. Before the seminar, the pastor and I were in conversation, and he mentioned that two years prior he had started on a walking program and changed his eating habits. He lost about forty pounds and never felt better in his life. He said these changes had made a dramatic difference in his quality of life. Then he shared with me what life was like before that.

> *The time has come for God's people to raise the bar, set the pace, and demonstrate before the world our appreciation to God.*

This pastor confessed that he had eaten whatever he wanted, ignored regular exercise, and did not consider stewardship of his body until he was faced with heart symptoms and had to undergo two angioplasty surgeries. When he accepted these health problems as a wake-up call, he felt the

Lord had given him a second chance. I'm certain his family and congregation are not only thankful to God for their healthy pastor, but also that they have been influenced by his example to make some healthy lifestyle changes of their own. Perhaps his influence was a major factor in my invitation to present my seminar.

Unfortunately, the body of Christ in general seems to have adopted our American cultural mentality toward self-indulgence regarding bodily appetites, along with the crisis mentality that says, "I am not going to change anything unless I have to change." This negligent attitude permeates all classes of people—pastors, church leaders, parents, youth, rich, poor, the famous, and the not-so-famous—causing the unnecessary and preventable health-related consequences.

> *Violating God's physical laws for the human body will bring devastating consequences.*

I can't begin to count the number of men and women who told me that if they had listened to the warning signs, they could have averted their current physical health problems, some of which were life-threatening. It doesn't matter what you have going on in your life, whether it is ministry, career, business, family, or friendship, if you are continually ignoring your health, you are a walking time bomb just looking for a time and place to explode.

God has uniquely designed and fashioned your body in a way that it can withstand abuse, neglect, and misuse for ten, twenty, even thirty years. But just about the time you are ready to cash in on all those abusive years that silently stole away your health by developing that business empire or climbing that corporate ladder so you could finally begin to enjoy the American dream, it happens. Without warning, that ugly face of ill health appears and sneers: "Now you are all mine."

Everything in your life comes to a screeching halt while you face the challenge of illness. Violating God's physical laws for the human body will bring devastating consequences.

Earlier I asked who was to blame for the generally poor physical condition of God's people. How about you? What is your level of commitment to God regarding your physical health? Are you being a faithful steward of His temple? Every one of us has a responsibility to God. We are accountable to Him for what we do with our bodies, inside and out. We should be faithful stewards of everything God has placed in our possession. If you have been unfaithful, there is no one to blame but yourself. If what I have said makes you angry or uncomfortable, it may be time to address these spiritual issues and make the necessary lifestyle changes. Remember that it's all about God and how much you love Him and desire to be a steward found faithful.

I challenge you to consider the stewardship, or lack of it, that you personally need to accept in order to bring glory to God in your body. I further challenge you to let your influence for good be an example to others. After sincere prayer for those you love who need to accept this challenge as well, go to them—your pastor, spiritual leader, family member, or friend—and encourage them to consider making some changes to improve their lifestyle and health. Don't worry about embarrassing them. Assure them you are concerned for them because you love them.

Your body, God's temple

Before you proceed to the practical application of the principles for health we have discussed, take the time to search your heart to determine what changes need to be made in your life. Ask God to forgive your neglect of His temple and to give you His grace to change. Set your mind on honoring Him with your body so He can use you as a witness to bring others to His kingdom. When His glory fills the temple, it becomes truly attractive to all who behold it. His ultimate design and destiny for your life can only be realized as you accept the responsibility for making your body the temple of God's presence.

Be bold. Be a pacesetter. Be focused, and enjoy the rewards for building a body for victory —it is a project requiring lifetime commitment and is filled with eternal value.

SECTION TWO

Builder's Plans

CHAPTER 5
Building Phase One: Interior Work

Building a body for victory takes planning. Just like building your own house, there are requirements that must be met during each phase of the building project until its completion. We have already established what must be done during the mental motivational phase. Your mental attitude makes up the foundation that you will need to build upon to get things started—and it enables you to stay focused. Now we are going to get into the actual building phase. But first, you will need to have a set of drawing plans.

I remember when Lori and I were considering getting a new house some years ago. We were not quite certain whether to buy a house or have one built, so we started off like most people by looking at models. Even that was a challenge for Lori, because I am not the typical shopper kind of person. If there is something I need or want, I go to the mall, get it, and get out of the mall as fast as I can. You don't catch me hanging out at malls.

But it was a different story when it came to looking for that perfect model home. I was amazed to learn that there were so many things to look for, and that not all houses are built from the same building plans or materials. This was a big investment—and we didn't want to make any bad choices. There were all the different building styles to take into consideration, such as contemporary, Victorian, or modern. We had to consider the elevation; did we want a two-story, single story, or split-level home? Then we faced decisions about color schemes and, of course, those model upgrades used to entice the buyer into buying the perfect dream house. Without fail, the models we liked the most and were really excited about were the ones that were too expensive for our budget. I wonder why that is always true. It is sort of like wishing you had the body of a beautiful model or sports figure but then realize that you don't have the same genetics to work with.

After traipsing through one model after the other looking for our perfect dream home, we came to the conclusion that since there were some ideas in each model we liked, and we couldn't get one model with all those features, we would custom build our own house. Choosing to custom build can be a real roller coaster ride if you don't know what you are doing, and we didn't. Eventually we found a custom builder with years of experience and the know-how to pull the whole project together. Best of all, he could capture our vision.

Throughout this section of the book there are several floor plans that I have drawn up for you to choose from for building a body for victory. I will take you step by step through each phase from start to finish and will supply all the materials and tools necessary for the job. Since I am a master builder, I know plenty of tricks of the trade that will help to customize your program. I will be glad to throw them into the deal at no extra charge.

WHERE TO BEGIN

The process of building our home was long and challenging at times, but once we determined the style of house we wanted, the number of rooms, the colors, what upgrades we could afford, and so forth, we asked the architect to make a set of drawings or floor plans. We soon discovered that before the house could ever resemble the home we envisioned, the building process had to start from the inside and work its way to the outside. It is important to understand that this same procedure is required in your spiritual life as well as in your physical life. True spiritual regeneration starts on the inside and is observed on the outside, as does true physical beauty.

We kept the final touches and the finished product locked in our brains to keep us stimulated, excited, and motivated as we pressed on through the laborious building project. Realizing that the mental picture we stored in our brains was the key to maintaining our focus helped us endure the building phase. Even though it didn't have much cosmetic appeal, we knew it was absolutely necessary. Without starting on the inside, there will be no outside results, no final product. Let's face it, how exciting is looking at the wiring and plumbing of a house being constructed? That's why it's hid behind the drywall! But nevertheless, in a newly constructed home *or in a body under construction,* the building process begins on the inside.

> *True spiritual regeneration starts on the inside and is observed on the outside, as does true physical beauty.*

If you want your body to function properly and be strong enough to resist illness and disease, plus look and feel in tip-top condition, it must first go through a healing process. In order for your body to heal, it has to rid itself of the toxins and debris that have been accumulating over the years. The first step you have to take is this: you must detoxify your body.

CLEANING THE INSIDE

Dr. Bernard Jensen, a leading holistic practitioner, has said this:

> In the fifty years I've spent helping people to overcome disability and disease, it has become crystal clear that poor bowel management lies at the root of most people's health problems. In treating over 300,000 patients, it is the bowel that invariably has to be cared for first before effective healing can take place.[1]

When talking about custom building your body, you need to consider the current condition of your health today. Without a doubt you have been polluting your body over time, whether intentionally or unintentionally. We all do this, so don't think that I am singling you out. This happens as a result of the way you live your life—your lifestyle. It happens because of the kinds of liquids you drink and because of the unhealthy food choices you make, consuming food with artificial additives and preservatives in them. By absorbing poisonous chemicals and pollutants into your body from the water you drink and the food you eat—and even from the air you breathe, your body becomes a toxic dump. Added to this are the medications you take (some of which are prescribed for you by a doctor), the lack of exercise you get, and a myriad of other things that affect your health. I am most certain your body is in need of some serious cleanup and repair work, so the first place we are going to start with is your "*in*vironment"—your colon. The term *invironment* was coined by Dr. Albert Zehr, a trailblazing nutritionist, who believed that life and death occurred in the colon.

The two best things that you can do for your body to start the healing process are:

- ***STOP POLLUTING!***
- ***START CLEANING!***

Knowing your body and how it works is vitally important. Being aware of what's going on inside your body is the place to start. In his book *Healthy Steps to Maintain or Regain Natural Good Health*, Dr. Zehr states:

> While the environment is the atmosphere and surroundings in which we live, the "invironment" is the atmosphere and surroundings inside of us. Just as our environment is being plagued by pollution, our invironment is no different. Unless we do two things, stop polluting and clean up the existing pollution, we will be faced with unnecessary health-related illnesses and eventually have a less than acceptable quality of life to the point that we experience premature death.[2]

As you understand how your digestive system operates, it will better help you to understand why I am placing so much importance on this phase of the job. Working from the inside out, colon pollution is directly related to nearly every illness and disease that occur in your body.

WHERE DOES THE FOOD GO?

I realize that elimination is not the central focus of our daily conversations. But as a result, it is probably the least understood of all our bodily functions. It is very easy to take it for granted until your health becomes an issue. Proper elimination leads to vibrant health and outward beauty, but when left unattended, it can lead to lack of energy, at best, and, even worse, to sickness and disease.

I remember my mother telling me to eat slowly. I don't know if she understood the magnitude of her statement or how eating slowly is directly linked to proper digestion or whether she just wanted us to take the time to enjoy her home-cooked meals. But chewing your food completely starts proper elimination in motion by causing an enzymatic action or breakdown of the food to occur in the mouth. When you swallow, your food goes directly to your stomach to be converted to a semi-liquid form called *chyme*. The stomach releases hydrochloric acid (or HCl) and other enzymes to help the digestive and elimination process.

Dr. Tom Spies, recipient of the American Medical Association's (AMA) Distinguished Service Award, reminds us, "All the chemicals used in the body—except for the oxygen we breathe and the water we drink—are taken through food."[3] The choices of food selections we make have a direct link to the way the bowel responds. Studies have shown that the regular intake of refined carbohydrates or sugars and the lack of sufficient fiber in the diet slow down the elimination process, increase the buildup of waste and fecal matter, and promote putrefactive bacteria.

Remember that your colon is a garbage bag, and you cannot afford to neglect it. Through neglect or ignorance thousands of people suffer from diverticulitis, irritable bowel syndrome, colon cancer, and many other chronic diseases. An unhealthy colon impacted with sugars, burgers, fries, and white-flour products is at the root of these poor health problems.

Do you have foul breath, feel achy, and experience sore joints or regular headaches? Consider that your colon and intestinal tract may be totally coated with plaque. That plaque, along with the infestation of parasites, may be what is making you feel lousy, weak, and unhealthy.

Most individuals start experiencing more digestive disorders after the age of forty because their bodies' enzyme production slows way down. That's why I highly recommend that you take digestive enzymes along with your meals.

After the food (chyme) leaves your stomach, it travels through the small intestine. This is where nearly all your nutrients are absorbed and assimilated into the body and transported into the cells for energy and good health. The chyme passes from the small intestine through the ileocecal valve into the colon, a large muscular organ five feet long, which is located at the end of your digestive tract.

COLON FUNCTION

Let me humor you since the topic is somewhat dirty. Imagine your colon (large intestine) being like a roller coaster that has lots of turns and bends. The passengers who ride the roller coaster are the chyme (which consists of ingested food and water), liver excretions, and other things. The ride begins at the cecum, located on your right side behind your lower abdominal wall. The car and passengers move up the ascending colon, propelled along by involuntary wavelike muscle contractions called *peristalsis*. Billions of friendly bacteria found in your colon begin breaking down the waste materials and indigestible nutrients like vitamin K and the B vitamins. The friendly bacteria also break down some of the protein into less complex substances.

> *Your colon is a garbage bag—you cannot afford to neglect it.*

As the car makes its first climb, it reaches the top of the ascending colon at the hepatic flexure, located near your liver. From there it makes a right turn and continues to climb as it goes across the transverse colon. Once it reaches the splenic flexure, the car makes a 90-degree downward turn and heads straight down the descending colon to the sigmoid colon and rectum, where all of the remaining passengers are to exit the car because the ride is over—right? Well, not always, or not always with regularity, if you know what I mean.

During the elimination and digestive process, the chyme is moved through the colon where good bacteria and moisture are absorbed. The matter that begins its downward journey through the descending colon is called *feces*. Toxicity and waste from your blood, as well as putrefying bacteria, are carried in the fecal matter to the sigmoid colon, the rectum, and then out of the body.

If your colon is healthy and operating normally, it will eliminate the toxic waste materials easily and regularly without strain. But if your colon is not in good operating condition, it will not eliminate properly. This causes those toxins in the feces to build up in your system and begin damaging and destroying your health.

All of the health professionals in the natural health field agree that most illnesses are linked directly either to a blockage in the colon or to poor bowel function. Well-known bowel specialist V. E. Irons claims, "In my opinion there is only one real disease, and that disease is autointoxication—the body poisoning itself."[4] It's the filth in our system that kills us. So, I'm convinced that unless you clean out your colon, you will never regain vibrant health.

Acccording to Dr. Norman Walker, a specialist in colon health:

> Good health not only regenerates and builds the cells and tissues which constitute your physical body, but also is involved in the processes by which the waste matter, the undigested food is eliminated from your body to prevent corruption in the form of fermentation and putrefaction. This corruption, if retained and allowed to accumulate in the body, prevents any possibility of attaining any degree of vibrant health.[5]

Dr. Walker concludes by saying, "Not to cleanse the colon is like having the entire garbage collection staff in your city go on strike for days on end. The accumulation of garbage in the streets creates putrid, odoriferous, unhealthy gases which are dispersed into the atmosphere."[6]

YOUR COLON AND YOUR HEALTH

Back in my elementary school days our teacher would show us how to mix white flour and water to make a paste. We were able to glue paper cutouts together with that paste to make ornaments. In much the same way, toxic slime from certain foods you eat builds up on the porous walls of the colon, actually plastering the walls like a paste.

> *Your congested colon becomes the culprit that is guilty of poisoning you.*

As the buildup accumulates over the years, your body can no longer absorb the nutrients from your food, or even nutritional supplements you may take, through those walls. Often, because of the buildup on the inner walls, there is barely enough space for food and fecal material to pass through. Believe it or not, most people are walking around malnourished and lacking energy because their colons are clogged, causing poor absorption. According to Dr. Walker, "The consequent result is a starvation of which we are not conscious, but which causes old age and senility to race toward us with the throttle wide open."[7]

AUTOINTOXICATION

Do you experience the blahs, not just once in a while, but day after day? Maybe you might exercise regularly, eat healthy foods, and even have regular bowel movements. But still you feel less healthy than what you know you should feel because of all the healthy lifestyle steps you are taking. Well, you could possibly be suffering from autointoxication.

If your colon is congested and has been plastered for a long time, it probably is not functioning normally. In fact, it cannot function normally! Your body cannot rid itself of all the rotting fecal matter because so much of it is impacted onto the colon wall. This slows down your body's ability to eliminate efficiently. Ultimately, your congested colon becomes the culprit that is guilty of poisoning you and producing toxicity throughout your entire body.

This condition of your colon also affects your body's ability to absorb nutrients properly. In fact, the small amount it is absorbing is toxic, because a congested colon is polluted and very toxic. Your entire digestive system becomes a toxic dump, and these toxins are carried via the bloodstream to other areas of your body, which contributes to a breakdown in their functions. This also causes your liver to go into overload as it struggles to filter your blood again. This condition will eventually lead to another host of health problems. Dr. Bernard Jensen says that autointoxication is "the result of faulty bowel functioning, which produces undesirable consequences in the body and is the root cause of many of today's illnesses and diseases."[8]

The colon seems to be able to endure this infectious and toxic condition without much pain because it lacks nerve endings. Unfortunately, many of these abnormalities are allowed to develop because they go unnoticed. Harvey W. Kellogg, MD, says, "Of the 22,000 operations I personally performed, I never found a single normal colon, and of the 100,000 performed under my jurisdiction, not over 6 percent were normal."[9]

According to Dr. Walker:

> If a person has eaten processed, fried and over-cooked foods, devitalized starches, sugar and

excessive amounts of salts, his colon cannot possibly be efficient, even if he should have a bowel movement two to three times a day.[10]

YOUR UNINVITED PARTY GUEST—THE PARASITE

If what I have just mentioned about your colon is not enough to get your attention, then how about the thought of having worms living inside your colon? Don't think that you are exempt, because you are not.

Approximately three hundred types of parasites thrive in the intestinal tracts of people in America today.[11] It is quite possible that you have a party going on way down there with uninvited guests that did not receive your VIP invitation. Let me help you understand the nature and motive of the parasite. Whether a microscopic single-cell parasite or a four-inch worm, these little parasites love to do two basic things: eat and make families. When it comes to dinnertime, they are first in line. Only after they are thoroughly fed will your body get a turn, getting only what is left over, mainly in the form of the parasites' excrement.

June Wiles, PhD and parasite expert, stated, "Parasites are vermin that steal your food, drink your blood, and leave their excrement in your body to be reabsorbed into the blood stream as nourishment."[12]

> *Approximately three hundred types of parasites thrive in the intestinal tracts of people in America today.*

These uninvited guests compound the problem of toxic backup into your bloodstream from fecal matter that is impacted in your colon walls. Now you must deal with the toxicity caused by these parasites also. This is some party you have going on inside—but hold on, it's not over. It gets worse!

IT'S A LONG RIDE

The *transit time* is the amount of time it should take for a healthy colon to transport the nutrients into the body for nourishment and then dispose of the toxic waste that remains. The volume of food and liquids ingested, as well as the condition of the colon, determines transit time. In a healthy colon, the transit time should be no more than sixteen to twenty-four hours. Elimination should occur once after each full meal. If the body takes longer than the normal transit time to eliminate the waste, then toxicity begins to build up. Once toxic buildup occurs, your digestive tract becomes a real breeding ground for parasites. Once these little guys have been fed, they begin looking for a home to raise their families. They love to multiply and produce lots of kids.

The faster the roller-coaster ride, the less time these parasites have to multiply. The average incubation period for a parasite is approximately thirty-six hours, so if your roller-coaster car is traveling at the prescribed sixteen to twenty-four hours, then you are in good shape. On the other hand, if your colon's transit time is that of the average American's, then you have serious problems. That's because the average transit time for people in America is ninety-six hours![13] Are you getting the picture now?

Parasites can gain entry to your body and become your unwelcome guests in many ways. It can happen as you shake hands or play with your pets. They can be transferred by adults, children, food handlers, and eating uncooked meats or raw fruits and vegetables. Parasites are easily passed around by millions of people each day, simply by coming into contact with one another. And, if you consider the millions of people who eat at restaurants every day, you can see how parasitic contact can become overwhelming. Usually if one member of your family has them, then everyone will get them.

Among children in temperate climates, the pinworm is the most common parasite. Overcrowded schools and day-care centers aid in passing these parasites around. These conditions have caused an increase in pinworm infestation in children. One child in six having pinworms used to be the norm, but now this infestation is up to an astounding 90 percent of children in America.[14]

While there are more than three hundred varieties of parasites, only about twenty-five varieties can be seen without a microscope. Those that can be seen without a microscope include pinworms, hookworms, roundworms, and tapeworms. These critters build colonies in the rectum and colon and cause them to be irritated and raw.[15] In the Southern states, the hookworm is most common. This uninvited body destroyer causes abdominal pain, diarrhea, malnutrition, apathy, anemia, and even underdevelopment in children.

The problem of parasites is much more widespread than the health professionals ever dreamed it could be. Centers for Disease Control experts point out that doctors are at a loss when it comes to the diseases brought on by parasites, because their training and schooling is very limited on parasitic infestations.[16] Doctors are reluctant to admit to microbial epidemics like parasites and clogged colons. Most people are ignorant of the health problems that can be caused by parasites. It is a medically known fact that impacted, clogged intestines and junk-filled and sugar-filled colons are the two major causes for the epidemic breakout of parasites. This condition of your *invironment* makes for the perfect climate for worms of all sizes to thrive.

Intestinal parasites and worms can cause you to be sick. For instance, if you are housing *Giardia lamblia*, you may end up doubled over with abdominal pain or vomiting, belching, feverish, and exploding diarrhea. Unfortunately, antibiotics do not affect the *Giardia*.

Having intestinal parasites or worms may cause you to have a greater susceptibility to weight problems. Parasitic infestation is due to the accumulation of undigested food and impacted food in your colon. That condition lends itself to the buildup of entire colonies of parasites, which destroy the normal digestive functions. Consequently the body cannot assimilate or digest foods properly. Many parasites do not penetrate the intestinal wall, but they leave your bloodstream full of their excrement. If they cannot enter your intestinal region, they can still dump toxins in your body and can challenge your immune system.

"LET ME OFF THIS ROLLER COASTER!"

By this point you are probably screaming, "What can I do?" You need to cleanse and detoxify your colon. To cleanse and detoxify your colon you should follow a cleansing system that has the ability to scrub the walls of your colon, remove the impacted matter, and restore it to normal function and regularity. I will give you more information about this in chapter seven, and I would recommend that you read about my Body Genetics INNER OUT Colon Cleansing and Detoxifying System in Appendix B, "Dr. Joe's Health Pack."

Keep in mind that if you do not have a bowel movement three times daily, then you are considered clinically constipated. If you eat two or three meals a day and only eliminate once every two or three days, it stands to reason that something is wrong—where do you think that food is going? You guessed it—it's staying in your colon. I remember feeding my daughters when they were infants. As soon as I finished with their feedings, I heard them grunting and watched their faces turning red as they made a mess in their diapers. Why? Because their colons were operating efficiently.

Most people assume that by taking a laxative (natural) they

are cleaning their colon, when, in actuality, they are only expe-riencing a loose bowel movement. One can have regular bowel movements and still not have a healthy, functioning colon. Only after your colon has been scrubbed clean of mucoid and fecal matter buildup can it function normally and absorb foods efficiently, eliminating the garbage regularly.

After a colon cleansing, your energy will increase because your body can absorb nutrients from your foods and supple-ments, your mental alertness will be keener, your skin tone and color will return, plus you will have satisfaction of mind that you have done the right thing for your health.

Once you have cleansed and detoxified your colon, there are additional ways to maintain a healthy colon to enhance a healthier life.

STOP POLLUTING AND START CLEANSING!

Avoid the "four whites."

To stop polluting your body, I strongly recommend that you get rid of what I call the "four whites" from your diet—white flour, refined sugar, salt, and fat.

White flour—White flour is dead flour, and it kills any prod-uct that is made with it. It provides empty, useless calories. You cannot easily digest white flour products, and besides contrib-uting to poor health, they are clogging your colon. White flour is a major contributor to weight problems, including low blood sugar, because your body treats white flour as sugar. When it is eaten too often and too much, the body experiences an over-insulin response, which contributes to a slow metabolism (the very thing you need to have running at high speed for weight management). Consequently, white flour interferes with the weight-loss process.

Let me show you something. God created the wheat in the fields perfect in its total composition. It lacked nothing and did not need to be fortified. The problem with wheat is that it fell into the hands of the food manufacturers. In the process of getting that beautiful white flour to your dinner table, all the fiber is stripped from it. During its destructive journey, a bleaching process is necessary, which destroys the nutrients. In obvious acknowledgment that good things have been removed, manufacturers then add some synthetic nutrients and call it "fortified, enriched" flour.

> *White flour is dead flour, and it kills any product that is made with it.*

Many innocent shoppers assume that all the products on grocery shelves are good for them. But that is not true. The food manufacturers have stripped the fiber and nutrients from the once healthy wheat, added a couple useless nutrients, and called it *enriched*—only to keep it on the shelves in your grocery store. If cockroaches have enough sense not to bother eating it, why shouldn't you?

Maybe you have always associated health issues like low blood sugar, diabetes, and child obesity as issues resulting only from overeating candies, chips, and ice cream. Well, think again. White flour and white-flour products fall in this category, too. Do yourself and your family a favor, and do not buy any more white-flour products. Try eating Ezekiel bread (sprouted grains and wheat), millet bread, spelt flour, and rice flour. Besides being good for you, these products are compatible with all blood types. Other alternative choices are buckwheat, barley flour, or 100 percent rye bread. If you eat wheat bread, keep it to a minimum. If you love pasta, try spelt, rice flour, and Jerusalem artichoke pasta as alternatives.

Refined sugar—Refined sugar (table sugar) is found in all candies, pastries, cookies, pies, sodas, sweetened iced tea, doughnuts, ice cream—and the list goes on and on. Refined sugar is not digestible. It contributes to tooth decay, obesity, depression, hyperactivity, and hypoglycemia; it weakens the immune system; it contributes to cancer; and much more. Does this sound like something you would intentionally put in your mouth?

An interesting irony is the fact that many parents reward their children for obedience or achievement by giving them sugary treats made with white flour and sugar. But because of the effects of those sugary treats, the child's health spirals downward and that award-winning child suddenly becomes hyper and out of control—the complete opposite of what parents are trying to do. Over time the child shows difficulty focusing and listening in school and can no longer simply relax. So out of desperation, the parents accept the recommendation of their pediatrician, who prescribes antidepressants and hyperactivity medications for that child. Not only does the child remain loaded with sugars, which are causing the problems, but he also becomes continually more toxic from the drugs, which will never be able to fix the problem. What kind of futures will those children have?

> *Refined sugar contributes to tooth decay, obesity, depression, hyperactivity, and hypoglycemia; it weakens the immune system; and it contributes to cancer.*

Table salt—Salt is also called *sodium chloride* because it consists of about 40 percent sodium and the rest chloride. If you eat a diet high in salt, it is also usually high in sodium. Sodium is a double-edged sword. It is a key element for maintaining proper bodily functions, and when taken in normal amounts (1,500 mg per day), it regulates proper metabolic function. But when the levels of sodium are elevated, the body begins retaining water to create equilibrium between sodium and water. Likewise, when the body water is low (say, after exercise), the brain signals the thirst sensation so the person will drink water and bring back the equilibrium between sodium and water.

The average American diet contains too much salt. When the levels of sodium are high, the water level is also high, and the kidneys must remove excess fluid in the body. Over time, this overload on the kidneys may cause health problems such as kidney damage or even failure. Along with kidney problems, the retention of water may stress the heart by increasing the volume of blood it needs to pump. High blood pressure may be directly associated with high sodium consumption as well. As an alternative for that salty taste bud of yours, consider using sea salt or kelp.

Bad fats—Not all fat is the same. Some fats are harmful when over-consumed, yet others enhance your health. To understand this, let's look at the three types of fat: saturated fat, monounsaturated fat, and polyunsaturated fat.

Saturated fats are typically solid at room temperature. Most of these fats come from animal sources, such as red meats and whole-dairy products like butter and cheese. Vegetable oils high in saturated fats are coconut oil, palm oil, palm kernel oil, cocoa butter, and hydrogenated vegetable oils, all of which contribute to trans fatty acids. Saturated fats tend to raise your total cholesterol count. They are difficult to digest and play a major role in the development of coronary heart disease.

Monounsaturated fats are generally found in vegetables and remain liquid at room temperature. A primary source of monounsaturated fats is olive oil. These were formerly termed "neutral fats," meaning they were neither good nor bad for people. But recent studies have shown an association with lowering the bad cholesterol (LDL) without lowering the good cholesterol (HDL).

Polyunsaturated fats are found in vegetables and stay liquid at room temperature also. These are the preferred fats to ingest. They are easily digested and act to lower LDL (bad cholesterol) values. Safflower oil, cottonseed oil, soybean oil, and corn oil are some examples of polyunsaturated fats.

I prefer virgin olive oil for cooking and salads as well as adding to various recipes. Do your best to avoid the oils (fats) that work against your health, especially against your colon's health. Follow these important health tips:

IMPORTANT PRACTICAL LIFESTYLE CHANGES FOR MAINTAINING GOOD COLON HEALTH

Do this:
- Add fiber to your diet daily.
- Drink plenty of water (alkaline when possible).
- Maintain a healthy, low-fat, high-fiber diet.
- Include regular daily exercise.
- Reduce as much stress as possible in your life.
- Eat for your blood type.[17]
- Do a periodical colon cleanse (twice a year).[18]

Most people think that building their body is a matter of developing massive muscles. Developing healthy muscles is a part of the big picture, but building your body starts on the inside. By adding these practical, healthy lifestyle practices to your daily life, you will provide your body with the proper tools for maintaining a healthy colon for this part of the building plan.

Now let's look closer at phase two of the building process and see what plans and building strategies I have designed for you.

CHAPTER 6

Building Phase Two: Your Food Pantry

Throughout the building plans section of the book, I will be addressing several key areas for building a body for victory. Each area is intended to educate you and help you by drawing up a couple sets of plans to follow. These plans will cover food types, dietary supplementation, exercise and workouts, mental thoughts, stress, and relaxation. All of these building phases play a vitally important role in total body and mind health. Since eating is a universal practice, and for some a pastime or recreation, in which we all must involve ourselves, let's head over to the pantry and start sorting out plans for food types that best meet your needs.

Now that you understand the first step and importance of beginning your building project of a healthy lifestyle by cleansing your colon from phase one, we can move to phase two in the building project—food plans. By food plans I mean the overview of "plans" or approaches to eating from which you can choose to improve your health. The fundamental reason for eating is survival. While in some cultures, getting enough food for survival is still the goal of life, in most other cultures, eating has far surpassed the meeting of those basic survival needs and has become a social and recreational activity.

Eating is a universal activity common to every language, culture, and society. Eating may represent a favorite pastime for some, moments of celebration, intimacy, family bonding, sharing with friends or strangers, socializing, or just plain putting an end to the growling hunger pangs coming from their tummies for others. Nearly everyone has created a mental and emotional association with eating food. For that reason, there are many whose personal image and self-worth issues stem from the way eating is perceived.

> *The primary purpose for eating is to provide the body with the correct fuel to operate at its best for the longest possible time.*

Because eating is connected with one's emotions, these personal issues have caused strong propensities for developing eating disorders such as bulimia, anorexia, overeating, and emotional eating. A society that places so much value on the outward appearance of an individual's body shape has dramatically changed the original purpose for eating. This shift toward meeting psychological needs through food has replaced normal eating standards with a feeding frenzy we call dieting!

Along with these psychological issues surrounding food, many people now *live to eat* instead of *eating to live*, allowing their psyches to be consumed with culinary pursuits. I have only mentioned a few aspects of the tremendous mixing bowl of dietary practices or habits that people face. As a result of these and other "food issues," the simple, natural norm of nourishing our bodies has become quite complicated!

We need to revisit the primary purpose for eating, which is to provide the body with the correct fuel to operate at its best for the longest possible time. My purpose as your master builder is to deliver to you a "product" that is custom fit to your needs. For that reason, I am providing you with several different approaches to eating that I believe will make all the difference in your goal to build a body for victory, to be healthier, more vibrant, and to enjoy a disease-free life. These plans are not presented as diets in themselves, but as the basis for understanding the role of food in determining your health. They are not arranged in any specific order. They are only included to give you a variety of ways to choose your approach to eating, to meet your custom needs.

DIETARY FOOD PLAN #1:
EATING ACCORDING TO BLOOD TYPE

The first approach for eating that I am presenting represents my preferred plan of choosing foods compatible to your blood type and avoiding foods that are not. In my book *Bloodtypes, Bodytypes and You*, I present the scientific logic behind eating certain foods and avoiding others according to your blood type.[1]

During the last eight years that I have personally incorporated this plan for eating, I have experienced wonderful benefits of weight management, controlled blood sugar levels, maintenance of low cholesterol levels, and living without the digestive discomforts associated with poor digestion and assimilation of food, to name a few. I am also convinced about the effectiveness of this approach to eating because of the thousands of people who have followed my prescribed eating plan and have shared their wonderful results with me as well. Most confirm that they experience improved energy levels, better digestion, less illness, improved illness profiles, weight loss, and overall wellness and health. So I am very comfortable in encouraging you to adopt this approach to eating.

The significance of your blood type

In my book *The Answer is in Your Bloodtype*, I cite extensive research done during World War I by researcher and physician Ludwik Hirszfeld and his wife, also a physician.[2] With access to large numbers of soldiers from many nationalities, they decided to carry out blood group tests for research purposes. They knew that for any findings to be validated, they would need reliable statistical results from testing large numbers of different population groups, along with precise ethnic description of their subjects and of their places of origin. They tried to test at least five hundred members of different population groups.

The results of their research established the main outlines of the world's distribution of the ABO blood groups. Their research also provided foundational information needed for the establishment of the science of population genetics, which gives scientists valuable information that helps guard against genetic tendencies to disease in individual patients.[3] Subsequent researchers have been able to establish an undeniable link between diet and disease. For example, as information in succeeding research was compiled according to blood types, it was discovered that people with blood type A were dying at an alarmingly young age from heart disease and cancer. People who were blood type O were living well into their eighties and nineties, some with disease but many without suffering any affects of illness.

Research indicates that diet is a major culprit for disease. For example, since blood types A and AB do not tolerate meat well, it is predictable that people with those blood types who live in America's "red meat culture" will live shorter lives than others who can tolerate more meat. While all blood types are susceptible to heart disease and cancer, the number one and two killers in this country, research shows that blood types A and AB die at much younger ages from these diseases than blood types B and O.[4]

For more convincing research findings regarding the advantages for eating according to your blood type, refer to my book *The Answer is in Your Bloodtype*.

Instinctive eating

In my book *Bloodtypes, Bodytypes and You*, there is a chapter entitled "How to Become an Instinctive Eater." I coined the phrase *instinctive eater* as it applies to making food selections compatible to your blood type. As a person eats correctly for their blood type, their body responds very positively, healing and improving their digestive system. In most cases, the former digestive disorders and discomforts associated with poor digestive function and that may have plagued the individual for years are eliminated within days to weeks.

The evidence of knowing whether or not the foods you are eating are actually helping can be determined by listening to your body's responses. The opposite is true as well; your body will react negatively to foods to which it is not compatible. Unfortunately, it is impossible to determine which foods affect you negatively unless you have "tuned in" to your body's responses. The best way to achieve that awareness is to avoid the foods listed that are not compatible to your blood type. Those foods may be contributing to poor digestion and assimilation, enhancing potential illnesses and disease and interfering with your body's energy production and its ability to lose weight. You will never know until you start making food selections that are compatible to your blood type and avoiding the ones that are not. That is how you become an instinctive eater!

Since eating is a necessity for good health, you will always depend on the type of fuel you ingest to achieve your optimal health. That is why it makes sense to eat what your body can most proficiently utilize. The relentless search of so many people for the right way to eat is evidence to me that people are not in touch with their body's responses. To help you avoid flipping around from one diet concept to another and wasting your time and energy, I have included here an overview of an accurate dietary floor plan, custom designed for your blood type.

	GUIDELINES FOR YOUR BLOOD TYPE			
TYPE	**BLOOD TYPE O**	**BLOOD TYPE A**	**BLOOD TYPE B**	**BLOOD TYPE AB**
FOODS TO EAT	Animal protein, foods rich in vitamin K, beef, mozzarella cheese, pinto beans, artichoke, broccoli, greens, figs, plums	Soy beans, tofu, green tea, grouper, cod, salmon, soy cheese, soy milk, lentils, broccoli, carrots, romaine lettuce, spinach, blueberries, blackberries, cranberries, prunes, raisins	Meat in moderation, lamb, venison, cod, grouper, farmer's cheese, feta cheese, mozzarella cheese, kidney beans, lima beans, navy beans, soy beans, broccoli, cabbage, collard greens, mustard greens, pineapples, plums	Limited to small amounts of animal protein, turkey, cod, mahi-mahi, navy beans, pinto beans, soy beans, oat and rice flours, collard greens, dandelion greens, mustard greens, figs, grapes, plums
FOODS TO AVOID	Pork, wheat, corn, lentils, navy beans, cabbage, brussels sprouts, potatoes, melons, oranges	Animal fat, meat or dairy products, meat-and-potato diet, kidney beans, lima beans, navy beans, Duram wheat, eggplant, peppers, tomatoes, cantaloupe, honeydew melons	Chicken, American cheese, ice cream, wheat, white and yellow corn, pumpkin, tofu, persimmons, rhubarb	Chicken, duck, all pork and venison, clams, crab, haddock, lobster and shrimp, kidney and lima beans, white and yellow corn, peppers, guava, mangoes, oranges

This is an abbreviated list, so for more complete information about eating according to your blood type, I recommend you read my book *Bloodtypes, Bodytypes and You.*

DIETARY FOOD PLAN #2:
ALKALINE/ACID ASH DIET

After reading about the significance of your blood type to your diet, you are aware that certain food types contribute to good health while others can actually contribute to poor health. Aside from the logic of the blood type diet, did you know that some foods actually create an environment in which disease and illness develop? I am not referring to what is commonly called "junk food," which certainly can destroy good health. It is a fact that even wholesome foods like vegetables and fruits, though more importantly, protein sources, can be detrimental to health.

In order to understand the role of foods that cause disease, we have to discuss the baseline of your physical makeup, which determines your health. I'm referring to what happens to your health at the cellular level as a result of the types of food you eat. The premise for this discussion is based on the fact that certain food types affect your body's pH balance.

You may be aware that the term "pH balance" applies to your body's acidity/alkalinity measurement. The pH (potential for hydrogen) factor measures the acidity or alkalinity of a solution and is an all-important point of reference in measuring one's current health and determining the potential of future health. Your pH values are measured on a logarithmic scale from 0.00 (acid) to 14.00 (alkaline), with 7.00 being the point of neutrality, which is neither acidic nor alkaline.

For every stage of illness and disease, from acute to chronic, your body's pH level is the primary factor of consideration. An acidic environment for your tissues and cells creates the environment in which disease can develop. Since the majority of people tend to have an acidic pH level, you should have an awareness and concern for being overly acidic. Unfortunately, many people are not aware that they are developing an acidic condition until the body starts employing its natural alert system by sending out painful warnings, in the form of symptoms.

Your body's natural survival mechanism works to protect you from disease by creating an alkaline buffer to neutralize acid buildup. Certain types of food work in concert with your body's protection mechanism to ensure its health against the ill effects of high acidity, or acidosis. Other food types actually work against your body's protection efforts and contribute to creating a pH imbalance, leaving an acid ash on tissues in your body.

It is important to remember, as you pursue a healthier, more vibrant lifestyle, that the innate healing potential in your body always pushes your physical health toward the "balance point" of ideal pH, known as a state of homeostasis. A state of homeostasis for the body can be considered a condition of physiological balance where healthy functioning cells work synergistically with the systems and organs of your body, causing them to operate in harmony with each other. The result—health.

> *Your body always pushes your physical health toward the "balance point"—homeostasis.*

When you consider how different everyone is, for example, in skin color, body types, blood types, and other individual traits, it only reinforces the awe of how wonderfully mankind has been designed. Just take a glimpse beneath the largest organ in the body—the skin—and you will become even more impressed with your body. As you investigate your body's design, you will soon discover that, as different as we are, we have this in common: we are all made up of trillions of cells. The composite design and health of these cells are what make you and me who we are. Yes, you have your own DNA and genome codes, but your primary baseline for existence is found in your cells—and we are, in this aspect, universally the same. The healthier you can keep your cells, the greater your expectation for a longer and healthier life.

The way to ensure that your body has healthy cells is to create a bicarbonate (alkaline) buffer system to protect the cells from becoming overly acidic. Acidity is created largely by the food types you ingest, although, as we will discuss, other lifestyle factors are also involved. Fortunately, the body has been fashioned to create this buffer system automatically, as long as there are needed reserve materials from which it can draw. You might say that the body naturally puts itself into a "survival mode" when it determines there is a dangerous condition developing.

The body has natural alkaline reserves, in the form of stored sodium, calcium, potassium, and magnesium. Without you even being aware of its protection mode, your body will tap into these buffer reserves every time you become acidic or develop a state of acidosis. It is a natural way for cellular fluids, known as *extracellular* and *intracellular* fluid, to maintain an alkaline/acid balance in the body.

The downside occurs when the body has used up all its alkaline reserves. That is when it triggers the body's natural alert system to send out warnings in the form of symptoms; at that point you may discover that you are in real trouble with your health. For example, a body's pH that is overly acidic (registering well below 7.0) may send out symptoms of gallstones, pain, explosive bowel movements (chronic diarrhea), or the development of cancers.

It is important to keep in mind that your body does

not make mistakes; it always fights to protect itself. It has been marvelously wired to lean toward the balance point, or homeostasis. It is programmed to protect itself by doing what it has to do so you will stay alive, whether or not its protective "symptoms" leave you feeling comfortable. To better understand the sophistication of your body's ability to protect itself, let me explain what potentially can happen to your gallbladder when your pH becomes overly acidic.

The gallbladder and gallstones

When there is a proper relationship between the bile salts, cholesterol in the gallbladder is in liquid form. However, when there is a disruption in this relationship, the liquid form of cholesterol changes, becoming solidified and forming stones. If it is true that the body does not make mistakes, you might be wondering why the body would take the sodium from the bile and cause painful gallstones to develop in the gallbladder. I mentioned that the body naturally protects itself when there is a problem brewing. In the case of gallstones, the body was becoming overly acidic (acidosis), causing it to launch into its natural survival mode for protection. It does so by tapping into its alkaline reserves. In this case, the sodium from the bile was needed elsewhere in the body to create an alkaline buffer to neutralize the acid buildup in the body and to help restore a pH balance. Unfortunately in the process, the former liquefied form of cholesterol begins to crystallize, forming hard, jagged stones.

The forming of gallstones results in severe bouts of discomfort and pain. Yet, the body is "forced" to create this condition because of the need to save your life by curbing acidosis caused by your eating habits. Again I make the point that your body will always do what is required to save your life. Unfortunately when pain persists, it generally sends you running directly to your doctor. Once under the doctor's supervision, you will probably be advised to consider surgery.

The question that must be answered is, *Will the surgery fix the gallbladder?* The answer is a resounding *no*. Why? Because the surgery is not reconstructive surgery but involves a removal of the gallbladder—a cholecystectomy.

Once the gallbladder has been removed, the pain is gone and you are relieved, but the root problem still exists: your body is still too acidic. The surgery did not resolve the problem; it only relieved the symptoms. In the final analysis, you just gave up a part of your body to surgery that was meant to stay intact and contribute to your overall health. It is likely that the problem could have been solved by correcting your pH balance.

> *Keep in mind that your body does not make mistakes; it always fights to protect istself.*

After removal of the gallbladder, the body does not stop trying to protect itself from the threat of acidosis. It stays in survival mode. However, since it has depleted the sodium reserves that could help move you toward pH balance, the body starts to pull from the next available mineral, calcium, to help create the alkaline buffer needed to balance your pH. Where do these calcium reserves come from? You guessed it—your bones. The survival mechanism of the body starts leeching calcium from your bones. I told you the body doesn't necessarily care whether you feel comfortable or not; its primary concern is to keep you alive by protecting itself.

Now, should you remain acidic, the body will continue to leech the calcium from your bones, causing decalcification. If the condition persists long enough, you will be dealing with a whole new set of problems, including weakened and brittle bones commonly referred to as osteoporosis. You could probably take medication for this condition, but regardless of how many pills you take or the quantity of lotion you apply, you have not addressed the root of the problem—you are still acidic. What can you do to reverse these conditions and deal with the root problem of disease? Better yet, how can you prevent these conditions from developing in the first place?

Lifestyle issues: acid vs. alkaline

To avoid the onset of ailments, diseases, and illnesses or to expect restoration to good health, you have to protect your cells from acidosis. It is said that we don't die of *disease*; we live or die at the cellular level. That is because the healthier the cells, the healthier the individual. The wisdom of this assumption is clearly to learn to take care of your cells.

There are several health destroyers that contribute to being overly acidic, including stress, negative thinking patterns, physical work, and exercise, as well as the foods you eat. For most people, acidosis is not caused by one factor but is a culmination of many different issues relating to your lifestyle.

You may be thinking that you are in deep trouble because you have plenty of stress in your life. Who doesn't? With the daily demands of today's society, many people get caught in a vicious cycle of a lot of work and no "play." This can often lead to anxiety and exhaustion, which is the perfect combination for stress to set in and an increase of acid buildup in the body.

It is a fact that people are controlled by the way they think. Thinking patterns do not only determine the outcome of their decision making, but they also have a direct effect on their physical health, especially as it relates to acidosis.

Another factor that lowers your pH levels, causing your body to be overly acidic, is excessive physical work or exercise. As you perform laborious physical work in your occupation or follow your exercise program at the gym, your body produces a lactic acid buildup, which is easily detected by the muscle soreness that accompanies the workout. Too much exercise will contribute to the imbalance of your pH, particularly if your body is already acidic.

Our main consideration here, however, is the role food

types play in contributing to your body's pH balance. As I mentioned, certain food types will leave an acid ash in your system, which contributes to a buildup of acid in your body's tissues. Other food types will leave an alkaline ash that helps contribute to neutralizing the harmful acid buildup.

There is a significant difference between acid-ash-producing foods and alkaline-ash-producing foods. Acid ash leaves behind minerals that must be neutralized before the body can dispose of them. The food types that produce acid ash are grains, dairy, and meats, which are high in the minerals phosphorous and sulfur. Your body is capable of handling these acidifying minerals, but in moderation. Food types that produce alkaline ash, leaving alkalizing minerals the body uses to neutralize excessive acid buildup, are vegetables and fruits. To summarize, eating more acid-ash-producing foods creates an accumulation of acid in your tissues, resulting in your pH being overly acidic.

As I discussed, to resolve the threat of acidosis, your body will go into its natural survival mode, tapping into the alkaline mineral reserves to neutralize the acid buildup. If you continue to eat more foods that leave an acid ash than alkaline ash in your cells, your body will eventually deplete its alkaline reserves, resulting in severe acidosis, developing an environment where disease can potentially form. This unhealthy condition can be prevented and reversed if you replenish the reserves with alkalizing minerals from alkaline-ash-producing foods.

While this is a simplistic overview of the complexities of your body's functions in regard to your pH balance, this basic understanding of the potential health problems and health protection available by addressing your pH balance represents an eating plan that can contribute to better health.

Testing your pH

Determining your urine pH indicates how well your body is responding to the foods you ate the day before. If you eat acid-ash-producing foods, your urine pH reading the next morning should read somewhere around 5.8 to 5.5. This acid reading shows the most favorable physiological response to acid ash foods and indicates that you have alkaline mineral reserves available. Should this reading change over time by becoming alkaline (over 7.0 pH), it may indicate that your alkaline mineral reserves in your body are very low and need to be replenished. You can do this by drinking ionized water (alkaline water), eating more alkaline-ash-producing foods, and/or by taking dietary mineral supplements. Remember that the goal is to maintain a pH balance in the tissues for maximum cellular health, which is directly related to overall health.

You will discover that testing your body's pH is something you can do yourself. You first need to purchase pH paper test strips, which are available at your local pharmacy and very inexpensive. A popular brand name is pHydrion Papers. The paper that registers between 5.5 and 8.0 is most suitable. You will want to see if there are fluctuations in your urine pH readings day to day. The testing process with the pH papers is quite simple. You can test as often as you wish, but many prefer to test daily for a two-week period.

An example of how to test for your pH can be found on page 90.

Another test to determine how well your body is functioning as a whole is called the saliva test. Your saliva represents all of your internal fluids, which are normally alkaline.

Your saliva pH changes very slowly over time, so you don't have to test it daily. By testing your saliva pH before and four minutes after eating, you get a read on how well your internal pH balance is coming along. You may test the saliva pH every two to three weeks, which is sufficient enough to let you know of your progress. Your saliva should test alkaline.

Put the paper strip in your mouth (on the tongue) and moisten the paper. Then compare the color of the paper to

THREE-DAY MONITORING
Day One
1. Begin monitoring urine pH with the first voiding in the morning after a day when you have eaten foods you usually eat. The numbers you get for day one will serve as a baseline. 2. Eat only acid-ash-producing foods (meats, grains, nuts, and so on). You may need to plan ahead for these meals if you ordinarily eat generous quantities of vegetables. 3. Drink only water, if possible. If not, limit coffee, tea, cola, or other beverages to 2 cups or less each day. Avoid alcoholic drinks and fruit juices.
Day Two
1. Repeat day one. Eat only acid-ash-producing foods. Limit water and other beverages.
Day Three
1. Resume your regular food selections after you take a reading on day two's food.

pH SCALE OF ACID REACTION IN THE BODY								
Acid								**Alkaline**
Total	Very	Moderate	Slight	NEUTRAL	Slight	Moderate	Very	Total
0	1–2	3–4	5–6	7	8–9	10–11	12–13	14

the color chart on the dispenser that comes with the pH paper strips. Keeping a simple journal with the date, time of day, reading before meal, and four minutes after that meal, will help you keep on track with your internal progress.

Alkaline-ash-producing foods

This food plan calls for selecting as many alkaline-ash-producing foods as you like on a daily basis, constituting approximately 75 percent of your total food choices, leaving 25 percent to acid-ash-producing foods. If your pH balance tested in the acidic range, you need to understand that, without changing your food plan, your body will continue down that path until you experience acidosis. At that point, the cells really start losing their level of energy for strengthening your body. The imbalance created begins to weaken your resistance—the immune system. Ultimately, disease sets in, and eventually your body will shut down.

Choosing this approach to eating is imperative if there is hope for reversing all types of disease, including cancer. It also serves as a preventative strategy for maintaining good health. The natural alkaline minerals that neutralize acid in the body will prevent common illnesses and restore the body to good health. This food plan, consisting of a daily diet high in alkaline ash-producing foods, is a perfect fit if you are:

- Physically active
- Eating a high-protein diet
- Under constant stress
- Dealing with negative emotions/thoughts
- Concerned with maintaining a pH balance
- Planning on being alive and well for many years

It is important to understand that the body does not become ill overnight; neither can health be restored in a day. In the field of natural health, we naturopathic doctors believe it takes a minimum of three months to restore an individual's health to normal. To begin this healing process, your body needs to first of all be detoxified. Then it must receive proper nourishment, dietary supplementation, and appropriate exercise to be restored to good health, along with proper mental attitude.

Listed below are a variety of alkaline-ash-producing foods. These are live foods and leave an alkaline mineral residue (ash) on your tissue, which neutralizes the accumulated acids in your body. This healthy residue will store as a reserve if not needed immediately.

ALKALINE-ASH-PRODUCING FOOD LIST				
FRUITS		**VEGETABLES**		
Apples	Oranges	Dried beans	Green beans	Rhubarb
Apricots	Peaches	Beets	Green peas	(dried)
Avocados	Pears	Broccoli	Lemons	Rutabagas
Bananas	Pineapple	Brussels	Millet	(green)
Blackberries	Raisins	sprouts	Mushrooms	Sauerkraut
Cherries (sour)	Raspberries	Cabbage	Muskmelons	Soybean
Dried figs	Strawberries	Carrots	Potatoes	greens
Grapefruit	Tangerines	Cauliflower	(sweet)	Spinach (raw)
Grapes	Watermelon	Celery	Potatoes	Tomatoes
Limes		Chard leaves	(white)	Watercress
		Cucumbers	Radishes	Other:
		Parsnips		Goat's milk

Acid-ash-producing foods

Before I list acid-ash-producing foods, let me point out to you that the main dietary culprit responsible for building acid accumulation is *protein*. People who eat a high-protein/low (or no) carbohydrate diet may drop unwanted adipose fat tissue and feel good about the way they look, but over time they will be worse off than they may realize. The acid residue that is left on the tissue from consuming an excessive amount of dietary protein actually congests the cells and reduces the pH levels, causing them to become dangerously toxic.

This cellular congestion and toxicity disrupts the osmotic pressure that exists inside and outside your cell membrane. Once this delicate balance of pressure is upset, the cells will retain water or fluid in an attempt to neutralize themselves and return back to normal. This phenomenon is referred to as *dilution*, which is the body's automatic response whenever there is an unusually high concentration of any substance found in the cells. The osmotic balance is restored, but the result is fluid retention.

Dietary protein is essential for a healthy body. When the amount taken in is excessive, your body has to produce more energy metabolically to process the protein than the amount of energy it receives from the protein. That's why eating a late-night, high-protein, peanut-butter-and-cracker snack can keep you awake until the wee hours of the morning. The body is working overtime to process the protein, when it should be rebuilding its reserves by resting.

If a diet high in protein is continued for a length of time, it may cause the body to deplete its sodium reserves (remember the gallbladder issues), which will then result in a demand placed on the body's other alkaline reserves. Left unchecked, the body will eventually deplete its other natural alkaline reserves: calcium, magnesium, and potassium. If you are not replenishing these alkaline minerals to help neutralize the tremendous acid buildup their lack creates, you can expect your health to take a dive until you do.

Do I think high-protein diets are good for losing weight? They are not good for maintaining proper long-term health, unless the acid residue that the protein leaves on the tissue is neutralized. To perform the pH balancing act, you will need to add those alkaline-ash-producing foods listed above. Of course, their addition to your daily diet moves you away from the high-protein/low-carbohydrate diet. It also gives you a better opportunity of being healthy while losing weight over the long term. This is another reason I prefer eating foods compatible to one's blood type.

The following list of acid-ash-producing foods comes primarily from protein sources—poultry, fish, dairy products, and grains. A few vegetables and fruits listed in the "other" column also produce acid residue in the body.

ACID-ASH-PRODUCING FOODS			
MEAT/ SEAFOOD	**DAIRY**	**GRAINS**	**OTHER**
Bacon	Butter	Barley	Blueberries
Beef	Cheese	Bran (wheat)	Cranberries
Chicken	Eggs	Bran (oat)	Plums
Codfish	Milk (cow)	Bread (white)	Currants
Corned beef	Yogurt	Bread (whole wheat)	Prunes
Haddock		Cracker (soda)	Honey
Lamb		Flour (white)	Peanuts
Lobster		Flour (whole wheat)	Peanut butter
Pike		Macaroni	Walnuts
Pork		Oatmeal	Carob
Salmon		Peas (dried)	Corn
Sardines		Rice (white and brown)	Lentils
Sausage		Spaghetti	Squash (winter)
Scallops		Wheat germ	Sunflower seeds
Shrimp			
Turkey			
Veal			

While not exhaustive, the food type lists above are complete enough to help you with your decision-making process for customizing your meals and snacks to fit your specific needs. As you consider the pH balance food plan, you will create opportunity for improving your health, strengthening your cells, ridding your body of toxins, and preventing the onset of unforeseen illness. To custom design your own meals or snacks, simply pick and choose which food types and groups you prefer. Along with an understanding of the blood type approach to eating, accepting the importance of maintaining a pH balance will make your potential for a healthy life much better.

The next dietary food plan is probably the most popular of all—the weight-loss plan.

DIETARY FOOD PLAN #3:
WEIGHT LOSS

The topic of weight loss may seem, at least to some, as common as the nose on your face. Those to whom this topic is so well known I call veteran dieters. Veteran dieters are weight-loss seekers who follow every weight-loss diet plan to the extreme, then stop when they can't lose any more weight and jump to the next one. If this describes your "food plan," I hope I can be of real service to you and show you that dieting is not—and never will be—the method of choice for successfully losing weight and keeping it off.

The fact is, successfully losing weight is more related to a metabolic factor than to a particular diet to which you ascribe. The inability to lose weight is actually due to a poor BMR: basal metabolic rate. Your basal metabolic rate reflects the ability of your body to burn calories efficiently while at rest. When you are physically active for over ten minutes, your body will increase its calorie-burning capacity. The longer you stay active, the more calories your body will burn. Obviously, your body burns calories whether your lifestyle is physically active or sedentary, but it functions very differently in these two lifestyles.

The ideal condition for your body is for it to be able to burn calories efficiently when it is resting—twenty-four hours a day. If you think about all the hours you are non-active—sitting, driving, sleeping—you can see how important it is to weight reduction for your body to continue to burn calories during its inactivity.

An inefficient metabolic condition, or slow BMR, is caused by making the wrong food selections, by poor assimilation of foods, and by physical inactivity. A slow metabolism is measured by your body composition—the percentage of body fat vs. lean muscle tissue. A negative body composition (NBC) is a metabolic condition where the individual's percentage of body fat exceeds the desired range, while the lean muscle percent-age falls short of its desired range. I refer to this condition as being metabolically "stalled out."

IDEAL RANGES (% OF BODY FAT)
FEMALE: 20–23% (30%+ = clinically obese) MALE: 15–20% (25%+ = clinically obese)

A positive body composition (PBC) is the metabolic condi-tion of having a desired body fat percentage (or below), while having an elevated lean muscle tissue. This PBC enhances proper weight loss, while NBC interferes with it. The premise to successfully losing weight, then, is dependent upon how well your metabolism functions; how well you digest, assimi-late, and eliminate food; and, of course, the important factor of regular exercise.

Dieting is not the method of choice for successfully losing weight.

Successful weight loss is not a matter of sticking to a weight-loss program for the rest of your life, though some veteran dieters seem to gravitate to that approach. If you have become successful at losing weight and reaching your ideal weight for life, it was not a weight-loss program that did it for you. Though the weight-loss program may have been the catalyst that moved you in the right direction, your success came because you learned the keys to metabolic health. You learned which foods to eat, which foods to avoid, when and when not to eat food, how much to eat, and how to increase your physical activities to maintain metabolic health. All these dietary practices are the keys that play a vitally important role in developing and maintaining an efficient metabolism.

Dietary "termites"

It is important that you stay focused on the fact that it is your metabolism that is ultimately the key player responsible for helping your body to release stored fat in order to lose weight. It will also be important to learn to detect "termites" that can wreck your plans for building a beautiful body with a PBC. Just as a house can fall into ruin by the insidious work of these tiny enemies, if you haven't prepared your plans properly for a beautiful and solid structure, your health plans can suffer ruin as well.

The following dietary "termites" will eat away at your metabolic foundation and ruin the goals you have set for losing weight and staying healthy. They work against your body's efforts to develop a positive body composition. Some of them need more explanation than others. Preparing yourself with the understanding of how these culprits work will help you as you build a body for victory. Dietary termites will destroy the foundation of your body and health.

Termite #1: Which foods to avoid?

After my years of practical application in working with my own and other people's blood types, I am convinced that the positive and negative response to food, according to your blood type, is the most logical method for determining which foods you should avoid. I believe that this approach to choosing acceptable foods, with its definite link to life span, disease, illness, and weight loss, offers the key to foods that you should avoid as well.

> *Dietary termites will destroy the foundation of your body and health.*

Please don't take my word for it. Give it a try for thirty days to see if you experience the dramatic difference in your health that others have experienced. Keep in mind that no one fully understands all there is to know about our bodies, their physiology, chemistry, the effect the electromagnetic field plays on its functionality, along with all the other complexities surrounding the health of what we refer to as our physical "self." But the health improvement I have personally experienced, along with thousands of others with whom I have worked, makes the blood type approach to eating, I believe, the most accurate and individualized dietary practice I know of to date.

It is not difficult to determine for yourself the effectiveness of this approach to eating. Secure a list of "avoid foods" for your blood type, and simply do your best to avoid these foods for each category, including condiments, spices, and juices for thirty days (the rH- and rH+ factors do not play into the blood-type diet).[5] Let your body be the teacher; it won't let you down. If you don't begin to lose weight, feel better, have more energy, experience less digestive discomforts, stabilize your blood sugar, or even lower your cholesterol, then this approach is not for you. All that is required is that you be honest with yourself and do your best to avoid those foods listed in the avoid food category for your blood type.

The chart on page 99 lists food groups that actually CAUSE weight gain, according to your blood type. You could begin by eliminating these foods for a while to see if the results you get are as positive as I predict they will be.

Termite #2: Refined sugar

Refined sugar is not a macronutrient. It is a nonnutritious, health-damaging element that has continually increased its presence in the daily diet of nearly every American and of millions of people in many other cultures as well. Refined sugar (table sugar) is not a serious problem when it is consumed in *condiment* portions. Unfortunately, for most people sugar has become one of the largest components (if not the largest) of the average American diet (approximately 150 pounds of sugar yearly). In such quantities, sugar is very problematic, threatening to destroy the delicate balance of sugar and insulin and resulting in damage to organs and tissues alike, causing life-threatening disease.

FOODS THAT CAUSE WEIGHT GAIN PER BLOOD TYPE			
BLOOD TYPE O	**BLOOD TYPE A**	**BLOOD TYPE B**	**BLOOD TYPE AB**
Corn—slows the metabolism **Cabbage, cauliflower, brussels sprouts**—inhibit thyroid hormone **Mustard greens**—inhibit thyroid production **Lentils**—inhibit improper nutrient metabolism **Navy beans, kidney beans**—impair calorie utilization **Wheat gluten**—slows the metabolism	**Meat**—stores as fat, increases digestive toxins, and digests poorly **Dairy foods**—inhibit nutrient metabolism **Kidney beans, lima beans**—slow metabolic rate and interfere with digestive enzymes **Wheat**—overabundance impairs calorie utilization	**Corn, lentils**—hamper metabolic rate, inhibit insulin efficiency, and cause hypoglycemia **Peanuts**—hamper metabolic efficiency, cause hypoglycemia, and inhibit liver function **Sesame seeds**—hamper metabolic efficiency and cause hypoglycemia **Buckwheat**—inhibits digestion, causes hypoglycemia, and hampers metabolic efficiency **Wheat**—slows digestive and metabolic processes, causes foods to store as fat, and inhibits insulin efficiency	**Red meat**—stores as fat, is poorly digested, and creates toxicity in the intestinal tract **Kidney beans, lima beans**—cause hypoglycemia, slow metabolic rate, and inhibit insulin efficiency **Seeds**—inhibit insulin efficiency **Corn**—causes hypoglycemia **Buckwheat**—decreases metabolism **Wheat**—decreases metabolism, is an inefficient use of calories, and inhibits insulin efficiency

Termite #3: High-carbohydrate/low-fat diets

Besides choosing the blood-type approach to making food selections for weight loss, I would strongly suggest that you minimize your consumption of carbohydrates and fats. Not all carbohydrates and not all fats cause a problem; some will even contribute to losing weight and/or being healthier. Carbohydrates, proteins, and fats are considered macronutrients, which are necessary for meeting your body's nutritional needs and maintaining a healthy body. As such, they should be consumed daily.

However, beginning during the early 1980s and into the 1990s, the high-carbohydrate/low-fat/low-protein diet was promoted as the way to go, according to many "experts" in dieting. Though I didn't ever buy into that concept, I do not believe you should go to the other extreme, removing all carbohydrates and reducing your diet to nothing more than high protein and fats.

To add to the promotional confusion of Americans regarding high-carb/low-fat diets, food manufacturers tried to capitalize on the trend. They produced sugary (though fat-free) snacks, marketing them as low-fat (therefore acceptable) foods for the dieter. Some even indicated that, because it was fat free, you could eat the whole box; you didn't have to worry about gaining weight. What they didn't tell you was that the contents of the box was laced with sugar as the primary ingredient. Without understanding how that sugar affected their metabolism, many did not realize why they could not lose weight, or in some cases, why they continued gaining. They didn't realize that the refined sugar they were eating was converted to fat and stored in the body, not to mention the other negative consequences greater quantities of sugar have on the body.

An interesting phenomenon took place during the time that high-carbohydrate/low-fat diets and foods were in vogue. Greater numbers of health conditions involving mood swings, depression, and blood sugar problems began to surface. I believe that to a large degree, most of today's blood sugar problems (hypoglycemia, hyperglycemia, and diabetes) as well as emotional depression, mood swings, and most major health problems, including the big one—cancer—are all linked to the many years of overconsumption of refined sugars.

To attempt to treat these "emotional disorders," science created legal chemical drugs like Prozac, Zoloft, lithium, and other mood stabilizers that stampeded the marketplace. Do you think there is a connection between diet and mood disorders? I do. Men and women are given these dangerous chemicals to help them calm down so they can cope with life's issues—please! I am convinced that the root problem to their bouts of depression and mood swings (even in children) is the overconsumption of too much refined sugar.

Cut out the refined sugars and refined flour for one month, and see how much better you feel and how much clearer your thinking processes are. Remove them for two or three months, and reflect on how much easier it is to cope with life's issues. In addition, I strongly suggest that you remove all the refined flour and refined sugar products from your children's lunch boxes and their afternoon and evening snacks. In fact, while you are at it, cut out the sugar-filled juices, too. It won't be very long before those "little brats" are transformed into respectful, well-behaved, darling little angels.

Don't be surprised if the behavioral problems like the alleged attention deficit disorder (ADD) or hyperactivity disorders and other alleged diseases become nonexistent. The rewards will be many for the mom and dad who regulate the nutrition of their children. First, your life will have less stress at home. Your children will have a better chance of being well focused, more in control of their actions, less apt to have fits of anger, and less likely to face child obesity problems. They will also become chemical-free because you won't need to continue using dangerous drugs such as Ritalin. Isn't removing refined sugars and refined flours from your family diet worth the results?

Termite #4: Fats

Another dietary "termite" that will play havoc with your foundation for a healthy body is saturated fat. Consumption of saturated fat will raise your bad cholesterol (LDL) blood lipid levels and interfere with your weight-loss progress. This fat type comes from animal foods and is easy to recognize, because it solidifies when exposed to room temperature air. You probably have seen a bowl of chicken or beef noodle soup after it sits at room temperature for a while where the liquid form of fat—oil—turns into solid form. I remember eating my mother's notorious homemade chicken noodle soup, particularly on the second day when it had to be reheated. She believed the flavor that made her soup so delicious came from that grease (fat) that solidified at the top of the soup. Flavor or not, I insisted that she scrape off all visible fat before she warmed the soup.

I suggest that the next time you make some homemade chicken or beef noodle soup, you let it sit overnight in the refrigerator before eating it. By scraping off the solidified fat you can minimize your saturated fat consumption. Remember to cut away all the visible fat on a cut of meat from the meat market or when ordering it in a restaurant—leaner is best! Keeping consumption of saturated fats to approximately 10 percent of your daily calories is probably a safe range. I don't think in the real world you are going to get it down to 0 percent.

There are good fats (oils) you should add to your diet. These are polyunsaturated and monounsaturated oils (fats), which work on your behalf. They provide your body with usable fats that can help offset artery-clogging plaque by contributing to raising your good cholesterol (HDL) lipid levels. Nuts and seeds are good natural sources for these healthy or good fats, as are virgin olive oil, omega-3 and omega-6 oils, flax and flaxseeds, along with some varieties of fish. Though these are healthy fats, consuming them in too great a quantity will interfere with your weight-loss goals. Still, they are healthy and should be a part of your diet. If you consume approximately 20 to 25 percent of your diet from the good oils (fats), you should be able to maintain a healthy balance of fats with those least favorable ones.

Termite #5: Feedings

"When to eat?" "When not to eat?" "How much to eat?" These seem like fair questions to ask. Of course I could never give you the exact answer, because we are all different. For example, we all have different metabolic rates, difference in digestibility (digestion and assimilation of food), different intensities of physical activities, and different work schedules, along with other lifestyle factors that affect each of us differently. However, in spite of our differences, I can give you some general guidelines in answer to these questions, which can become a part of your building plans.

I remember the way our family meal planning was designed and followed when I was kid. Typically my mother was in charge of the "pantry business" and would wake us up to a before-school breakfast around 6:00 a.m. She had already been making my father's breakfast and his sack lunch for work, so that between 5:30 a.m. to 6:30 a.m., Monday through Friday, breakfast was served at the Christiano homestead.

Lunchtime varied somewhat because my three siblings and I were in school and all had different school lunch breaks; generally ranging from 11:00 a.m. to 12 noon, as did my father's lunch break at work. I honestly can't tell you what my mother's feeding times would be, which would have had to fall after the hustle and bustle of getting her family out the door. Supper for all of us was at 5:00 p.m., unless my father's work schedule changed. Every evening, between watching TV and bedtime, we enjoyed some "goodies" that my mother made.

Weekends were an entirely different story. Saturday breakfast could have been anywhere from 6:30 a.m. for my father, who worked six days a week, to 9:30 a.m. for us, because we slept in.

Lunch for all of us was still around noon, and supper was at 5:00 p.m. as usual. Sunday feeding schedules were practically set in stone. Breakfast was at 8:00 a.m. and was a family event because we all went to church afterward. Lunch rolled in around 1:00 p.m., right after church. Supper at 5:00 p.m. and before-bedtime goodies remained on the same schedule as on other days.

It is interesting as I look back and see that my parents kept a basic structured timetable when it came to meal planning and feeding times. As a rule breakfast was never skipped, lunch was important, and supper was a family event. Even the goodies we ate in the evening during TV time were a family or social event.

However, things changed as we grew older and became involved in different activities. I participated in sports after school and on Saturdays, so supper at 5:00 p.m. was not possible during my high school years. When I was not involved in sports, I was busy with my paper route or working part-time jobs, so my feedings were not regularly scheduled. At the same time, my body's demands became greater. If you consider the workload of sports, part-time jobs, and a full day at school, you can understand why I would have a greater appetite. Besides that, I began lifting weights when I was thirteen years old, which added additional demands on my body. With all these activities, feedings not only became more important in their frequency but also in quantity and quality.

As you compare your childhood eating experience with mine, you will understand how different everyone's life and lifestyle are. Determining the best time to eat, when not to eat, and how much to eat will be different for everyone. Maybe you can relate to my very structured meal schedule as a child, or perhaps you recall a not-so-structured feeding system. In either case, we often pass on to our families those practices we learned from our upbringing.

However, the times in which we now live are much different from when we were growing up. Too often, the fast pace of our lifestyle is dangerous to our health. We are in such a hurry that sitting down as a family and eating a meal in a quiet environment is often unheard of. As a child, life seemed much simpler, the pace much more laid back. At least in my childhood experience, mealtimes were exciting, because our meals were cooked from scratch and enjoyed as a family.

Then there were my father's classic remarks about our feeding system, like, "When it's time to eat, you better be home on time because the kitchen closes when we are through eating." His golden rule at the table resounded equally as strong: "Take all you want, but eat all you take." Then there was his mild rebuke: "If you open that refrigerator one more time I'm gonna put a lock on it." And his ultimate complaint: "All I wished for when I got married was someday to have four children; instead I ended up with these four bottomless pits to feed."

For us, eating was not a kind of reward or a mechanism with which to cope with life; it was the reality of a necessity for maintaining health. Even my father's classic statements provided a sense of security and peace to our family that many families today do not enjoy, perhaps due to single-parent homes or other situations. While we celebrate our differences in society, there are some basic principles for feedings that can guide you to successful weight-loss efforts or to improved health in general. You may want to consider these as you build a body for victory. The following guidelines are basic and will serve as a starting point, which can be modified to meet your unique differences:

1. Don't skip breakfast.

You are breaking a fast (break-fast), and your body needs nourishment. Breakfast time can vary for everyone and needs to accommodate your schedule, but don't go without eating. Wholesome carbohydrates like fresh fruits are good to have, especially when you are just getting things moving. However, stay away from commercial fruit juice—it's loaded with sugar.

Use a juicer, and include vegetable juicing as well if you want to have juice. You can also have a protein meal, protein drink, or protein snack. Avoid any of these if refined sugars and/or refined flours are among the top three ingredients on the nutritional label. Keep the total of refined sugar down to a near "condiment" or "trace" portion.

2.   Midmorning snack

You may want to consider eating a midmorning snack as a means to maintain your blood sugar level, especially if you are diabetic, hypoglycemic, or are experiencing bouts of low blood sugar. If you are dealing with any of these conditions, I would suggest a protein-type snack such as a handful of nuts with a piece of fruit. Again, no refined sugar or refined flour products (like doughnuts). Sometimes it is necessary to eat several small meals throughout the day as a means of keeping your metabolism revved and maintaining a constant blood sugar level. This is referred to as "grazing." On the other hand, it is not imperative that you always have a snack; by listening to your body and the signals it sends, you will be more instinctive with your eating habits.

3.   Don't count calories.

I am not an advocate of counting calories. It comes from the dieting mentality, which causes you to become dependent on a set of rules instead of learning to listen to your body's needs. The best way to determine how much you should eat is to follow this simple rule of thumb: eat when you are hungry, stop when you are satisfied (not stuffed); don't eat if you are not hungry.

Many people cope with their emotional issues by reverting to food. I know—I'm an emotional eater. Please remember that whatever you may be dealing with emotionally, the resolve you need will not be found in the pantry. Try prayer, relaxation, rest, exercise, or any positive means to address those emotional issues—not eating.

4. When NOT to eat

If you are trying to lose weight, there are some key times during the day that you should and should not eat. Late-night eating, which includes any time closer than three hours before bedtime, will interfere with your body's ability to metabolize food and lose weight. In fact, you will most likely gain weight when making a habit of eating at that time.

Also, if you want to get a jump on your fat-burning progress, try doing your cardiovascular workout immediately after getting out of bed in the morning and BEFORE eating anything. With the exception of water, your body is carbohydrate depleted in the morning because your body has just gone through a fasting period for seven to ten hours. By immediately exercising, your body will tap into the fat reserves it needs for energy to exercise much sooner than if you had eaten before exercising.

5. Drink plenty of water daily.

I am an advocate of drinking sufficient water daily. I find this practice to be a challenge to many people. I have had clients who never drink water because they can't stand the taste of it or they want something fizzy going on in their throat when they drink. That's because they are used to drinking soda, which, by the way, will never quench your thirst or meet your hydration needs. If you need a little fizzy action, try some sparkling water—but do drink plenty of water.

By hydrating your body daily you will enhance your body's ability to lose body fat, and you will support the kidneys and colon for proper assimilation and digestibility of food. I suggest that you drink one 8-ounce glass of water every waking hour per day or until you reach one-half your weight (in ounces). Drinking water does not include drinking tea, coffee, or other beverages—it means drinking water. If at all possible, I strongly recommend alkaline or ionized water that has an alkaline pH. (For more information on alkaline water, see Appendix B, "Dr. Joe's Health Pack.")

DIETARY FOOD PLAN #4: MEAL-REPLACEMENT DIETS VS. TRADITIONAL DIETS

I would like to share with you some information on the validity of meal replacements, particularly if you are interested in losing weight. Of course, I am aware that I am presenting to you the ideal world for cultivating a healthy body for victory. The wisdom God has given me through the years helps me to understand there is a vast chasm between the ideal world of health and the real world where most people live. In fact, in most instances, these two worlds may never intersect because they are at opposite ends of the spectrum.

Let me explain. The ideal world says, "Eat small, nutritious meals throughout the day, never skip breakfast or other meals, drink plenty of water, exercise daily, take supplements, get out in the sunshine, think positively, avoid all stressful situations, prepare all your meals from organic food sources," and on and on. The real world says, "Whoa, Dr. Joe, I can't stand eating first thing in the morning, and anyway, I don't have time for breakfast. Sometimes I don't eat lunch either. Exercise, who has time? Take dietary supplements? Who has the money for those things? Don't skip meals—right. Try following my schedule some day!"

Understanding this great divide between the ideal conditions for health and the real situations in which people live, I have learned to compromise. Instead, I present my beliefs and what I know is ideal for you to be healthy and successful in reaching your goals, and, in the process, I have learned to bend and meet you halfway. Since the only absolutes in this life are God, death, life, and taxes, I have taught myself to lighten up a bit so I can be better in touch with my clients and their real-world issues. So let me help you intersect these two "health worlds"—the ideal and the real. Consider the following research documenting the validity of using meal replacements in the "real" world, where it is not possible to enjoy fresh-cooked meals from organic foods several times a day.

The March 2001 issue of the *Journal of the American Dietetic Association* includes a year-long study of sixty-four overweight women, ages eighteen to fifty-five, who wanted to lose 20 to 40 pounds and maintain the weight loss.[6] The women claimed they couldn't change their eating habits, no matter how hard they tried. Half the women were given a standard 1,200-calorie meal plan that you have probably all memorized by now. The other group was told to replace all three daily meals with a liquid shake containing 220 calories, supplemented with fresh fruits and vegetables, to total 1,200 calories per day.

The result? After the first three months, both groups of women lost 3 to 6 pounds of body fat without losing lean muscle mass. But after one year on the program, the women using the meal replacements maintained their weight loss, while the other group regained the lost weight. Sound familiar?

Another study of one hundred overweight people (twenty-one males and seventy-nine females, ages thirty-five to fifty-five), published in the August 2000 issue of *Obesity Research*, also sheds a favorable light on the use of meal replacements.[7] For the first three months, half the participants followed a 1,200- to 1,500-calorie diet, while the other half had two meal replacements per day, plus one balanced meal. At the end of the three months, the traditional dieters lost an average of 1.7 pounds and the group using meal replacements lost an average of 7 pounds.

At this point, both groups were asked to use one meal replacement and one snack replacement each day for the next four years. At the end of the study, the traditional dieters lost an average of 3 pounds, while the meal replacement group lost an average of 8 pounds. It appears that initially losing more weight helped the second group maintain their weight loss for a longer period of time. Both groups saw a decrease in blood sugar levels, but only the meal replacement group had lower triglycerides and blood pressure levels.

I was glad when I read the positive results of those studies because they helped confirm what I always believed about the use of meal replacements. Since I have always been an advocate of the use of meal replacements, I was happy to learn that not only do they help people lose weight, meal replacements also offer more hope for those who struggle with keeping the weight off that they lost. Unless you have experienced being extremely overweight as I was (at 305 pounds), you can't imagine what it is like to find something that brings hope.

The version of meal replacements I have developed may be different from others that are available, but they are worth investigating, especially if the success of your building plans includes losing weight. There are some very popular diet plans advertised on television or in the newspapers that include meal-replacement snacks or foods. However, I am more concerned about what nutritional value is in the meal replacement than just the replacement concept itself.

The weight-loss program I have developed, Dr. Joe's ThermoBlast Weight Loss Program, comes with delicious meal replacement snacks that meet all the nutritional requirements, which I insisted my manufacturer include. (See Appendix C for more information on ThermoBlast Meal Replacement Products.) They are compatible for all blood types, containing no wheat, corn, or artificial preservatives, and they are naturally sweetened. I place value in meal replacements not only for their immediate help in weight loss, but also for the long-term success they offer for those who struggle with maintaining their weight loss. They are especially helpful for those who habitually make the wrong food selections, eat wrong portions, and have a habit of skipping meals. Meal replacements may be another idea for you to consider as you look for the customized plan for your body.

SUMMARY

I think by now you should have a good idea of the importance of making healthy lifestyle changes, both for the short and long term. With the goal of building a body for victory, you were introduced to the building process in phase one by beginning on the inside, detoxifying and cleansing your body. Then we moved on to the second building phase, giving you several how-to strategies regarding food types and the link between your blood type, diet, disease, illness, and weight loss. You now have a variety of choices of plans for the pantry, which can help you create a healthy pH balance and utilize other building plans that can ensure the prevention of potential unhealthy conditions, diseases, and illnesses.

In phase three of this building process, we will explore several choices of supplemental plans to help fortify your body and health with needed nutrients. You will learn how this dietary supplementation should be added to the "mortar" for nutritional support.

CHAPTER 7

Building Phase Three: Dietary Supplements

As a young teenager in 1961, I began to take dietary supplements, paying for them out of the money I earned from my paper route and snow shoveling jobs. I recall reading books by Adele Davis, one of the pioneers of that time in the field of nutrition. Her books helped me understand the importance and value of adding nutritional supplements to my diet in order to build a healthy body. I have shared my involvement in sports and weight training, which demanded that I be strong and healthy.

Living in the suburbs of Buffalo, New York, I would make monthly trips like clockwork to a particular health food store located in a quaint area called Allentown, where hippie-like people congregated to drink coffee at the street-side cafés. I would purchase supplements and protein powders with my hard-earned money instead of spending it in frivolous ways as some of my friends did. Since those early years I have always considered nutritional supplements as an investment into my life. Thank God, I have enjoyed a very physical, energetic, and healthy life and am walking proof of the benefits of additional nutrition that these supplements provide.

PRESCRIPTIONS VS. SUPPLEMENTS

It has been fascinating to me to compare the patterns of life-style between people who run to the doctor and take medications for whatever ails them and others who decide to build a healthy lifestyle naturally, as we have discussed. I recall visiting one of my many aunts when I was a kid and how amazed I was, even as a young person, to see all the different bottles of medication she kept at her place at the kitchen table. The message to me was loud and clear: when you get old, you will have to take lots of medications.

The prescription pattern

Now, forty years later I am an aging boomer, and I still see the same pattern with older people who have developed the habit of taking medications for what ails them. When I visit my mother and stepfather, I notice that the majority of their conversations center around their health problems, the health problems of their friends, the medications they take, the cost of those medications, and their complaints about taking their medications. Their medications don't seem to make them better. And they keep adding new ones to those they already take. What's the deal? Why are the elderly still taking more medications but not getting any better?

Why are you taking medications that aren't making you better? If the medications the doctor prescribes are intended to be the remedy for health problems, why are kitchen countertops still loaded with medications? If they really improved health, it seems that there would be a need for less medication, not more. That would be the case—if it were true that medications could heal illness and disease. But it is not! The problem is that medications don't address the root problem that is causing their ailments; they just target symptoms of disease. Medications are nothing more than symptom stoppers!

To continue medication for symptoms for years without

seeing improvement in one's health, while believing one will get better, is about as plausible as believing a house that is on fire can be saved if firefighters just keep spraying water on the smoke. If you insist on treating symptoms, you are like firefighters spraying the smoke; you can say good-bye to your health and to your house!

Unfortunately, this loss of health is often not the fault of the patients who are taking their doctors' advice and trusting that the medication prescribed will make them better. What usually happens, however, is an increase in the pattern of medication when treating symptoms only. The doctor begins by giving you one prescription for a particular condition (symptom), then over time another is added, and another, until eventually you have a tray full of medications. If I were the patient, I would be asking myself, "If the first medication was intended to make me better, why all the additional prescriptions?" Could it be that the patient is not actually getting better, but in fact is experiencing a worsening condition, along with increased impact of the side effects caused by most medications? For example, people stay on blood pressure medication for years and yet still have elevated blood pressure. It seems logical to conclude that the medication is not "fixing" the problem—the root cause of the high blood pressure. It is simply a part of the prescription pattern.

> *Medications don't address the root problem that is causing their ailments; they just target symptoms of disease.*

I have a friend who had stomach problems for years and was taking pain medication his doctor prescribed. His doctor told him he would have to stay on the medication for the rest of his life. Well, my friend didn't want to believe that, so he would try, from time to time, to get off the medication. However, when he did, almost immediately the pain would come back.

He thought he was doomed to take the pain medication all his life. When he shared his dilemma with me, I suggested that he consider learning to eat foods compatible to his blood type. He agreed to try it.

Within two weeks, he contacted me to say he was eating according to his blood type and the pain was gone. Not only that, but he was saving approximately one hundred dollars a month that he spent on the medication. His relief came over two years ago. You can do the math—my calculations conclude that he has saved approximately twenty-four hundred dollars by not having to waste it on pain medication that was not making him better. Do you recognize the prescription pattern?

Supplement solutions

In contrast to the dismal prescription pattern, taking dietary supplements offers a totally different solution. As a naturopathic doctor, when I see a client who complains of having an illness or has been allegedly diagnosed with a disease, the first suggestion I make is to take specific dietary supplements that target the root problem of their symptoms, if need be. (Of course, I take a full evaluation of the patient before treating him or her.) The length of the illness and the impact it has had on the body will determine how long it will take to correct the problem.

While dietary supplements are not formulated to cure illness or disease, they are designed to provide the internal environment for assisting your body in the healing process. They help promote cellular health and systemic and organ function, and they assist in purifying your body through removing toxic buildup so that your body can heal itself and be restored to normal health as it was designed to do. In short, they offer a long-term solution.

We are all in need of additional nutrition. Healthy lifestyle changes include a change of mind or attitude about your entire makeup—body, soul (mind), and spirit. Supplements can enrich not only your physical body, but they can also enrich your thinking and your attitude. It is your brain that enables your body to build healthy, functional molecular structures. The brain operates like an electrical generator, allowing electricity to flow through your body, including the liver. The liver is dependent upon the brain's electricity for its supply of mineral energy, particularly calcium. When there is a disruption or short circuit in the electrical flow to the liver from the brain, the liver is deprived of its energy, which sets the stage for degenerative changes in the liver. Like a domino effect, the rest of the body's organs and systems are affected, and you have what is known as the onset of degenerative diseases.

The microscopic overview of chemistry in your brain is meant to point out that the most powerful causes of interference of electrical flow to your body from your brain are worry, fear, lust, self-centeredness, hatred, and bitterness. These negative mental exercises that block the flow of energy from your brain to your liver are responsible for nearly 95 percent of all degenerative disease.[1] As the Bible tells us, "As he thinks within himself, so he is" (Prov. 23:7, NAS).

Defective thinking has an effect on your body chemistry. If the ability of your mind to comprehend or understand is blocked, in a sense it has the potential of canceling your entire health program. From a physical perspective, the first stage of mental impairment begins with calcium deficiency. Combine that with a carbohydrate imbalance, which interferes with oxygen to the brain, and you have the makings of mental distortions, resulting in your thinking being unclear and full of anxiety or fear.

Make nutritional supplements a part of your lifestyle, and remember the word *prevention.* As you experience the many healthy returns from additional nutrition, you will discover your decision is a wise investment in your health.

In the beginning, contrary to the "one prescription" pattern, a patient may need more supplements to provide the healing nutritional environment for their condition. But as the body heals, not only are symptoms alleviated, but also the disease is gone, and the need for certain supplements decreases and is finally eliminated. This supplement solution is totally opposite to the prescription pattern, which ends in dependence on multiple medications.

> *It's all about investing in your health,*
> *not paying for sickness.*

Dietary supplementation is most effective as a prevention of illness and disease. However, it also provides the proper environment for the restoration of one's health by creating the nutritional baseline to maintain a healthy functioning body. In contrast, medications are designed to treat symptoms of disease; they cannot make you healthy! I understand that sometimes it may be necessary to take mediations to address an acute condition or to assist in the case of an emergency. But ultimately, the goal should be to eliminate medications as soon as possible, so your body can rid itself of their toxic effect, and to restore health with good nutrition.

Don't just take my word for it. Begin to examine the evidence for yourself. This information should be a wake-up call for you if you haven't considered taking dietary supplements, regardless of your age. It's all about investing in your health, not paying for sickness. Because I believe so adamantly in the necessity and benefits to your health of adding nutritional supplements to your daily regimen, I have developed "Dr. Joe's Health Pack," a list of the basic supplements that I believe every person should take to achieve optimal health. Please see Appendix B where I list each supplement and describe the benefits it can give you. You may also use the Web site address or the telephone number listed to get further information about each of these products.

DIETARY SUPPLEMENT BASELINE

In building the foundation of a house, reinforcement rods are added to the cement for strength and support; the cement alone is not strong enough to create an adequate foundation. In much the same way, the effectiveness of dietary supplements is limited; they cannot be completely responsible for your health. Though supplements can greatly enhance the potential for optimal health, they can't do it all themselves. They need your help.

Their health benefits can be maximized when synergy is created between dietary supplements and the mix of healthy living practices. Nearly all of us are potentially deficient in our balance of nutrition due to a litany of factors such as poor digestibility and assimilation of foods, a dysfunctional colon, or pH imbalance. In addition, by virtue of careless environmental practices, pesticides, chemicals, fertilizers, and waste materials are being dumped into our soil, water, and air. As a result, nearly all edible vegetation lacks the God-designed minerals and nutrients originally intended to help sustain the life of humankind.

So, even with your best efforts for healthy eating, you are likely to be deficient in minerals and vitamins. Even the natural aging process demands that we have more nutrition support in our diet to maintain and restore health. But, as important as dietary supplements are to your building plan, they do not stand alone. Taking handfuls of supplements without also practicing healthy lifestyle choices will not be effective for building a body for victory. For that reason, I have listed here the seven key lifestyle areas that need proper attention in order to experience optimal health. These areas will work in synergy for optimum health, making your dietary supplements effective.

SEVEN KEY LIFESTYLE AREAS

1. Diet
2. Drinking water (alkaline preferably)
3. Regular exercise
4. Rest and relaxation
5. Daily exposure to sunshine and fresh air
6. Physical activities
7. Positive thoughts

As you consider these key areas, decide how they apply to you. If you have not included them in your life, now would be the perfect time to begin. Developing the consciousness we are discussing toward your body, soul, and spirit as a whole will make it easier for you to make healthy lifestyle changes. A body built for victory will be the result of blending these lifestyle practices together with the proper attitude and motivation. The potential outcome for health is unlimited.

Understanding specifics

While supporting your diet with dietary supplements is a wise investment in your current and future health, getting started with supplements can be somewhat confusing. Our body's nutritional requirements vary due to a number of factors like our individuality: blood type, age, current state of health, activity level, level of stress, current weight, current medications, eating habits, and food choices. Nutritional goals are also different for each of us.

For example, if you are physically active, engage in recreational sports and activities, or follow a regular exercise program, it may be necessary to maintain a generous daily intake of protein to meet the extra demands placed on your body. If you are planning to lose weight or want to gain weight, there are specific supplements you can take to help you reach your goals.

I personally increased my magnesium and potassium intake to correct irregular heartbeats I was experiencing. In this way, taking dietary supplements can be very specific to your current need, as well as broadly based to cover general nutritional needs. Whatever your nutritional goals, please consider adding dietary supplements to your lifestyle to help you reach them.

If you have decided to explore the prospects of fortifying your body with sound nutrition, you will want to consider the basic floor plan that follows. I have made a brief list of dietary supplements and their descriptions that I believe will cover the bases for most people. If you have a specific health condition or are concerned about taking dietary supplements, please consult your physician or wellness expert before incorporating them into your diet. If you would like to discuss your specific dietary needs, go to www.bodyredesigning.com and click on "Ask Dr. Joe."

For our discussion, I have limited the dietary supplement baseline categories to:

- Digestion
- Colon health
- Diets deficient in vitamins and minerals
- Protein consumption
- Decline in hormone secretion
- Dehydration

These are categories related to our need for basic supplements that apply directly to the condition of your immediate and future health. They should be of great concern for you and your family. There are many other areas relating to dietary supplementation, nutrition, and illness, but these are listed for the purpose of supplying you with enough building materials necessary for developing a solid foundation.

Supplements that aid digestion

Are you aware that digestion begins in your mouth? That's why it is vitally important that you chew your food very thoroughly. As you do, enzymatic action takes place in your mouth, and enzymes begin breaking down the food into digestible morsels. Then, as the predigested food enters your stomach, additional enzymes are released and further digestion occurs, all in preparation for the food to enter into your small intestines where the nutrients can be absorbed into your blood stream and carried to your cells.

Unfortunately, as you age, your body produces fewer enzymes to aid in this digestive process. Consequently you not only experience digestive disorders and the discomfort they bring, but also you cannot get the nutrients from the food you are eating, which eventually leads to poor health. This lessening of natural digestive enzyme production seems to occur in individuals age forty and over. To compensate for this lack, I suggest that you start taking a digestive enzyme complex supplement before every meal.

Digestive enzymes not only eliminate digestive discomforts, but they also give the liver and digestive system a break, supplying what is lacking for proper digestion. A good digestive enzyme complex supplement will provide a variety of enzymes necessary for breaking down proteins, fats, and starches/carbohydrates, enhancing your body's uptake of nutrients and food assimilation.

Colon health

In phase one, "Interior Work," I covered the importance of a healthy colon as it pertains to a litany of health-related problems. These common, yet avoidable, problems—including liver dysfunction, degenerative diseases, headaches, achy joints, weakness, weak immune system, skin ailments, poor skin tone, bad breath, blood health, and cancer of the colon—are related to an unhealthy and dysfunctional colon. So make sure you do a colon cleanse at least twice a year. See Appendix B, "Dr. Joe's Health Pack," for more information on Body Genetics INNER OUT Colon Cleansing and Detoxifying System.

Staying regular

After going through colon cleansing and detoxification, it is necessary to take care of your colon on a daily basis. Maintaining healthy elimination and preventing constipation require a normally functioning colon. For that purpose, fiber is your best friend. Fiber helps prevent the buildup of waste and toxicity in your colon while contributing to lowering your bad cholesterol. Fiber also provides the bulk necessary for speeding up the transit time for proper elimination. (In chapter five we discussed in detail the importance of maintaining a healthy transit time in your colon of twenty-four to forty-eight hours.)

Vegetables, fruits, and grains like rolled oats and oat bran (plus plenty of water) will help provide the necessary fiber to your diet. A fiber supplement like psyllium husks plays a tremendous role in regularity and should be an everyday part of your diet. See Appendix B for more information on Body Genetics Psyllium Capsules.

Chronic constipation

Chronic constipation is very common these days and is a very dangerous condition. It contributes to illness and poor and abnormal colon function, causing toxicity buildup, which in turn may lead to serious health problems such as colon cancer. Many people experience chronic constipation, with no bowel movement for many days or even weeks. This painful condition can also lead to parasitic infestation. If you are suffering from chronic constipation, I recommend an extra-powerful herbal laxative that results in immediate bowel movement. See Appendix B for more information on Body Genetics Cape Aloe Capsules.

Daily multiple vitamins

As I have mentioned, prevention of illness and disease should be your goal when it comes to taking dietary supplements. By taking a balance of vitamins, minerals, and herbs, not only will you accomplish that goal, but you will also create a healthy safety net for optimal health. Taking a multivitamin every day is a means to supplement your diet with the nutrition that may have been lost from your food through over-heating, preservation methods, or contaminated food sources. I take daily multiple vitamins that are formulated for my blood type. See Appendix B for information about Body Genetics AM/PM Multi-Vitamins, a daily supplement formulated according to blood type needs.

Trace minerals

Since your body does not manufacture trace minerals, it is very easy to become mineral deficient. For that reason you need to supply your body with trace minerals. Adele Davis, my teenage nutrition guru, taught that if you traced any illness or disease back to its roots, you would discover the cause to be mineral deficiencies. Without trace minerals your body cannot absorb vitamins. I find that a liquid concentrated form is the easiest to use, allowing you to mix it with water, soups, drinks, or take it right from a teaspoon.

I have had great success in helping people dissolve bone spurs and avoid surgery simply by suggesting they take forty to sixty drops of liquid trace minerals for a thirty- to ninety-day period of time or longer if needed. Strong nails, fast nail growth, better hair condition, and more energy are just a few benefits you will experience when adding trace minerals to your nutritional regime. "Dr. Joe's Health Pack" in Appendix B includes information about Body Genetics ConcenTrace, a form of liquid trace minerals.

Calcium

Calcium is the most abundant mineral found in our body and a basic organic mineral essential for the function of every organ and gland. It is also vital for balancing the blood and tissue pH in the body. A deficiency in calcium is directly related to decalcification and, eventually, may lead to the development of osteoporosis. While calcium is the major mineral our body needs, it is the most difficult mineral to absorb. Calcium requires magnesium in a 2:1 ratio (calcium/magnesium) plus vitamin D_3 (cholecalciferol) to be assimilated properly in the body. Calcium comes from reef, stone, or shells like coral calcium and plants like green vegetables. Be sure to add those green vegetables to every plate of food at the dinner table.

Note: A pregnant woman requires five to seven times more calcium than a man does. To enhance your intake of vitamin D, try spending one or two hours in direct sunlight. Make it a habit of life to get out in the sun! And check out Body Genetics Coral Calcium and Mega Mineral Complex in Appendix B, "Dr. Joe's Health Pack."

Protein

Protein is essential for the health of your body, and it cannot function without it. It is likely that you are not getting enough protein on a daily basis. Increasing protein in your diet and lowering the carbohydrates will assist your body in losing unwanted weight. Protein is excellent for mental alertness as well. It is absolutely necessary for energy, immune function, heart health, muscle repair, and building of healthy muscle. Protein helps stabilize blood sugar, so if you suffer from hypoglycemia or bouts of low blood sugar, you can avoid "crashing" in the morning and afternoons with a proper protein supplement.

The majority of your protein intake should come from food sources, but eating protein is not always palatable or convenient. That's why I recommend considering a protein supplement in the form of a bar or shake. A protein bar or shake may serve as a meal replacement or an in-between-meal snack.

Soy protein makes a great shake and is especially beneficial for blood type A and AB individuals, while it is neutral for the O and B. Rice milk, almond milk, and goat's milk are also good alternative sources of protein. Some people, like myself, enjoy egg-white protein powders for shakes. Use a protein shake that is compatible to your blood type so you can get maximum assimilation and benefit from it. When I travel I always take my stash with me—protein powder and protein bars. "Dr. Joe's Health Pack gives you information about Body Genetics Protein Shakes and ThinTastic protein bars.

Hormone(s)—antiaging

There is nothing you can do about the clock on the wall as it ticks away in perpetual motion. So when it comes to aging, we have that in common; we're all getting older. But as we get older there is something we can do—we can slow down the aging process. I am referring to avoiding health-related conditions associated with aging such as increased body fat, loss of muscle tissue, decrease in libido and energy, elevated blood pressure, poor sleep quality, and poor appearance (skin tone), to mention a few. These common conditions associated with aging can be reversed or slowed down by taking human growth hormone (HGH), preferably in a homeopathic, oral form.

HGH, a natural hormone produced by the body, is critical during childhood and plays a key role in the entire development of the body, bones, muscles, and organs. However, the quantity of HGH that the body produces dramatically decreases as you age. HGH is produced naturally by your pituitary gland and other immune cells until you reach your mid-twenties. But by age eighty, it is virtually nonexistent in your body. The natural aging process that affects your overall health and quality of life is due in part to the lack of HGH in your body. Consider the effect of stress, which interferes with the production of human growth hormone production, on your life, and you can see why it's all downhill after you hit thirty years of age.

Since I have been taking this antiaging hormone supplement, recumbent human growth hormone (rHGH), it has helped me stay leaner, has improved my skin tone, and has given me the satisfaction of knowing that I am replacing what my body won't produce anymore. Even my mother, who takes it, comments on how well she sleeps. If you are over thirty years of age, male or female, I recommend that you consider adding rHGH to your dietary needs.

In addition to the lack of HGH production, many times the body has a difficult time releasing the HGH that is stored in the pituitary gland. Therefore, by adding a HGH-release supplement you can assist in the release of your body's store of HGH. I give you information about Body Genetics Homeopathic rHGH and HGH Release in "Dr. Joe's Health Pack."

Alkaline water

There are three basic causes for disease and death: (1) free-radical damage to cells, (2) dehydrated cells, and (3) acidosis. When you consider that the human body is made up of trillions of cells, it is logical that the healthier the cell, the healthier the individual will be. You may not be aware that it is the baseline solution (or liquid) inside and outside the cell that determines its health and function. When free radicals (impaired molecules) attach themselves to cells in the body, those cells break down and die. Depending on how long cellular damage has occurred, the degree of ill health will be determined. The particular disease or illness you will develop depends on where those damaged cells are located in your body—for example, liver, heart, or blood.

If the cells do not receive proper hydration (water) with necessary alkaline minerals, an imbalance in the cells occurs and the body falls out of homeostasis. Ultimately this condition may lead to a variety of diseases and eventually death. Additionally, when the intracellular and extracellular fluid pH level becomes acidic for too long, the body will experience a breakdown in organ function. As we have discussed, this condition is referred to as acidosis. Remember from our discussion of the alkaline/acid diet plan that acidosis can develop from foods that leave an acid ash on the tissues, from physical activities like manual labor and exercising, from stress and negative thoughts, as well as from chemical imbalances.

It is often impossible to eat a diet with 75 percent of fresh vegetables and fruits that are not devitalized from being overcooked or are not loaded with additives. That is why it is wonderful that, thanks to our advancements in the field of nutrition, we can drink a type of water that provides a constant flow of alkaline minerals, helping to neutralize any acid buildup in our bodies.

> *Implementing healthy lifestyle practices in concert with dietary supplements is the formula for building a healthier you.*

After studying the scientific research on the difference between acid water and alkaline water I have made a habit of drinking ionized (alkaline) water exclusively. Yes, I had to buy a machine, but it is worth the money it costs. This machine attaches to a sink faucet and restructures ordinary city tap water into chemical-free alkaline water. It not only filters out the chemicals that make our drinking water unhealthy, but it also retains all the alkaline minerals that are in the water: sodium, calcium, magnesium, and potassium. It also reduces the molecular size of the water by half and, through electrolysis and an electrical charge, drives more water (alkaline, not acidic) into my cells.

This alkaline form of water neutralizes the acid buildup from my exercise workouts and from the foods that leave an acid ash on the tissues. And it is chemical-free water. Alkaline water is a natural antioxidant, which counteracts the potential damage to my cells caused by free radicals. It supplies my body with plenty of alkaline minerals and assists in balancing my pH. Now when my diet is short on alkaline-ash-producing foods like vegetables, I am OK because I drink alkaline water. Please, drink alkaline water.

Everybody is drinking bottled water these days. As important as it is for you to hydrate the cells daily to keep them healthy and properly functioning, it is equally imperative that you know the type of water you drink. I have researched what kind of water is contained in most bottles. And I discovered that nearly all bottled water is acidic simply by doing a pH test.

I once attended a Natural Foods Expo in Washington, DC where my wife and I had our display booth. Next to us was one of the largest bottled water companies in the country, with mountains of stacked bottles of water to give to the public. I asked the doctor of the company (who was involved in the purification process of their water) if he could tell me the pH of their water. He said it was bioavailable. He could have said he didn't know and saved his credibility, but he didn't. Knowing he was dodging my question, I asked him if I could test his water in front of him and his national representative to find out. He agreed to my request.

Remember that a 7.0 pH is "neutral" and anything below that reading is "acid." Their infamous purified water measured a 4.8 pH. After the test, I turned to the doctor and said, "Sir, you are selling the general public purified, acid water." He and his representative turned and walked away. Since there is a direct link between your blood and tissue pH and the development of cancer and other known diseases, maintaining your pH balance is crucial to health. You should be concerned about the type of water with which you are hydrating your cells so that you do not contribute to an acidic condition in your body. Again, I encourage you to drink alkaline water.

If your budget prohibits you from purchasing an alkalizing machine (approximately $900), there is an inexpensive and easy way to alkalize your water. Put eight to ten drops of Body Genetics ConcenTrace, a liquid trace mineral, into 8 ounces of water to help raise the pH above 7.0. I use this method when I travel and alkalized water is not readily available to me. (See Appendix B for more information on Body Genetics ConcenTrace.)

Remember this dietary supplement baseline is not mandatory, nor is it exhaustive in scope, but it does provide a good foundation for basic supplementation. There are no magic bullets, potions, or lotions for improving your health. Implementing healthy lifestyle practices in concert with dietary supplements is the formula for building a healthier you. A healthy life is not limited to just your body, as we have discussed. It includes your emotions and thought processes as well. It encompasses the physical activities (positive), nutrition (what you ingest and digest), the thoughts you embrace like forgiveness, kindness, love toward others (positive thoughts), a positive focus (walking in victory), and connecting with your Creator (perfect peace of mind).

> *When you maintain positive thoughts, they become directly responsible for accomplishing every goal and desire you may have.*

We all are in need of additional nutrition. Make nutritional supplements a part of your lifestyle, and remember the word *prevention.* As you experience the many healthy returns from additional nutrition, you will grow in the wisdom as to why I perceive it as a wise investment in your health. (See "Dr. Joe's Health Pack" in Appendix B.)

NUTRITIONAL IMPACT OF YOUR THINKING PROCESSES

Earlier we discussed the importance of attitude when approaching the issue of building a body for victory. Your attitude has an amazing impact on the outcome of your decisions. You will also discover that the negative thoughts you hold on to not only impact your decisions but also directly affect your health. Let me give a short recap of attitude and then explain how negative thoughts may affect your health.

"It's all in your head," my mother used to say to me when I was coming down with a cold. She also said that when I expressed my fear of something, particularly if it was some-thing beyond my control. I recall as a young man discussing some of the heavy pressures in my work with my mother, like cash flow problems, accounts past due, deadlines, setbacks, the economy, and their effect on my sanity. Her typical response to my frustrations was, "It's all in your head." Then she added, "And if you let it get to you, I'll come over and slap it out of you." Now there's an approach you might want to try on someone for handling negative thoughts!

My mother's simple response to my fears was basically true. Our thoughts are very powerful. When you maintain positive thoughts, they become directly responsible for accomplishing every goal and desire you may have. They will inspire you to move beyond where you thought you could go. They are a vital part of the essence of peaceful and harmonious relationships between one human being and another. Positive thoughts are the intangibles necessary for all successful achievements, accomplishments, and victories; they are the stuff that develops a good attitude.

Conversely, negative thoughts may be very damaging in many ways. They have the power to prohibit you from accom-plishing your dreams and desires. They will rear their negative heads the moment you are challenged with some physical, mental, or spiritual assignment. Most opportunities for suc-cess are lost because of negative thoughts, particularly fear and self-doubt. Negative thoughts will destroy beautiful relation-ships in marriage, with friends, and in business. I believe that many people who are losing the battle in their thought lives will never reach their fullest potential. Their struggle between the negative and positive thoughts, perhaps unknowingly, with their inability to break away from the negative pattern of thinking, may be damaging to their whole life.

Think back to your childhood upbringing. Many people lived as children in an atmosphere where they were bombarded with negative commands from caretakers. Perhaps it is not fair even to blame the caretakers, because they are a product, as we all are, of a damaged human nature, more given to disobedience and foolishness than to making sensible choices for life. It is this damaged nature of a child that causes a parent to constantly feel the need to correct and direct the child. Parents spend much of their child-rearing years giving negative commands to their children like: "Don't touch that." "Don't go near the steps." "Don't eat that." "Don't yell at your sister."

Should the caretaker be a negative-thinking individual themselves, then the negative atmosphere may be more damaging to the child. How many of us have been told by caretakers that we would never amount to anything, that we were idiots or stupid? How many of us grew up treating others as we were treated, putting them down or mocking them? While those negative traits are a part of human nature, they were also reinforced by the negative commands from our childhood upbringing.

> *We had to embrace the positive thoughts that said, "I can, I will!"*

There is an old saying that goes like this: If a lie is told enough times it will eventually be perceived as truth. Applying that concept to your own thinking patterns and their effect on your self-esteem, but consider the times you backed down when faced with a new challenge. Why did you say to yourself that you could never succeed in a certain area, convinced that you were not capable of doing it? It may be because you have listened too long to the lies that said you were stupid, and they became truth to you. You chose to not believe in yourself. Letting go of those negative perceptions will be a life-changing experience, affecting every area of your life and health.

When I was a competitive power lifter, I was constantly challenged when faced with making a heavy lift that I had not made before. Obviously, it takes intelligent, progressive strength training and diet to reach your maximum strength. But a vital element to breaking the records, whether they be personal, national, or world records, is resisting negative thoughts and overcoming the mental struggle. As athletes, we had to reject every negative thought (fear or self-doubt) that tried to convince us we were not strong enough to lift that new amount of weight. We had to embrace the positive thoughts that said, "I can, I will!" Without winning the battle of the mind, we would never advance to lifting a greater weight, even though our muscles were capable of doing so.

Negative thoughts and your body

As we have discussed, negative thinking not only affects the outcome of the challenges we face in life, in relationships, and in our personal esteem, but it also directly affects our physical health. I would like to point out that nearly 95 percent of all disease and sickness starts in your brain.[2] The body and mind (thoughts and thinking process) are vitally connected to the issues of your health that are very real. This body, mind, and spirit connection is a physical reality.

It is a scientific fact that electrical frequencies and magnetism in your brain connect the thought processes to the building of healthy functional molecular structures. The brain operates like an electrical generator that transmits electrical currents, which flow throughout your body, including one of the most vital organs, the liver. Your liver is dependent upon the brain's electricity not only to receive its patterned frequencies for proper function, but also for the invaluable initial magnetic draw that allows the uptake of mineral energy, particularly calcium. When there is a disruption or short circuit in this electrical flow from the brain to the liver, it is deprived of this magnetism that is vital to your health. A downturn in function is caused in the liver, which sets the stage for degenerative changes to take place in the liver. Like a domino effect, the rest of the body's organs and systems, which interact with the liver, are affected, creating symptoms of one of the increasingly common "degenerative diseases."

I gave you that simple overview of physical chemistry as it relates to the body/mind and health connection to explain that disease and illness are direct responses to altering or short-circuiting the electrical flow from the brain to the liver. It is also a scientific fact that the primary causes for interruption of the flow of electricity from the brain to the liver are—you guessed it—negative thoughts. Negative thoughts filled with hatred, bitterness, unforgiveness, self-centeredness, lust, and greed (to name a few). Wow! Those negative-thinking patterns sound like the results of a damaged nature. Do you have any of these floating around your head? Are you choosing to hold on to them? Let me add another piece to this puzzle of body/mind connection to your health to give you the big picture.

These negative thoughts or defective thinking are the enemy of truth and have an effect on your body chemistry. If the ability of your mind to comprehend or understand is blocked, it will affect your ability to make proper judgments and will interrupt the benefits that come from healthy living changes.

By understanding the mind/body connection and how negative thoughts (not attitude) directly have an effect, it becomes obvious that the condition of our health has much to do with the negative thoughts we hold on to.

From the physical (body) perspective, the first stages of mental (mind) impairment begins with calcium deficiency. Calcium is manufactured in the body by the liver, making it more susceptible to interruption of electrical impulses from the brain, which is associated with negative thoughts. Combine the mind (negative thoughts) with the physical (body) conditions that interfere with oxygen to the brain, a carbohydrate imbalance, and you have the recipe for mental distortions resulting in thoughts of anxiety, desperation, and fear.

Negative thoughts or defective thinking are the enemy of truth and have an effect on your body chemistry.

If you ever read the biblical account of the twin brothers Esau and Jacob, you will see that Esau traded his birthright for a bowl of stew. I believe that Esau's response demonstrates the body/mind connection we have been talking about. My guess, as a doctor of naturopathy, is that Esau represented the classic example of someone who was struggling with severe low blood sugar or hypoglycemia. He may have been suffering from a carbohydrate imbalance from not eating, which leads to a lack of normal oxygen flow to the brain. This may have contributed to the serious misjudgment he made by his decision to give up his birthright

As the story goes, Esau the hunter had been out in the wild hunting. The Bible doesn't indicate how much time he spent out hunting, but he eventually returned to where his twin brother, Jacob, was making a stew. Esau confronted his brother and demanded some of the stew because he was famished. Jacob responded by asking for his older brother's birthright as a trade. Esau was willing to give up his birthright in exchange for satisfying his physical appetite. "What good is a birthright," he exclaimed, "if I die from not eating!"

This condition can lead to defective thinking and generally occurs due to a lack of peace because of negative thinking. Your mind will fall prey to anxieties, frustrations, guilt, phobias, depression, and the like when there is a lack of perfect peace.

If a person is cognizant of when he chooses to give in to defective or negative thinking and becomes willing to change the way he thinks, he will definitely experience improvement in his physical health. It doesn't end with improved physical health; he will also experience improved emotional and spiritual health as well.

At times, however, physical deficiencies can create negative thoughts. It doesn't matter what nationality, race, gender, or religion you are; everyone is affected by what I call a damaged nature or physical deficiencies that result in negative-thinking patterns. This damaged nature is a result of being separated from a personal relationship with God. Cultivating a relationship with God, accepting our need for a Savior, and repenting of our sin reintroduces us to the Prince of Peace, who can help us change our thinking patterns.

According to the Scriptures, God's nature or Spirit produces perfect peace. Maybe God had more in mind for us than we realize, with respect to the body/mind connection. The apostle Paul declared, "And the [perfect] peace of God, which passeth all understanding, shall keep your hearts and minds through Christ Jesus" (Phil. 4:7).

Paul prefaced that statement with this instruction: "Be careful for nothing; but in every thing by prayer and supplication with thanksgiving let your requests be made known unto God" (v. 6). Our Creator understands the vital connection He formed within us between the mind and body. I believe the Holy Scriptures in many cases are directed to the reader not only for spiritual matters of the heart and mind, but also in regard to the connection between the body, soul, and spirit. As triune beings, we cannot separate the unique functions between body, soul, and spirit. That is why the foods we eat, the thoughts we think, and the faith we have in God directly affect each other. It makes me wonder if born-again Christians, who confess faith in Christ, are not tempted by the enemy of their souls to ignore this connection for the destruction of their "temples."

The following is a list of helpful practices you can incorporate into your life to nullify the effects of negative thinking:

- Pray to God and meditate on His Word—for perfect peace.
- Forgive those who have trespassed against you—for you have been forgiven; liberate yourself.
- Fast from solid foods—healthy body/healthy mind and heart.
- Make wise food choices—healthy body/healthy mind.
- Practice relaxation exercises—to relax the body and the mind.
- Keep in check negative thoughts—let them go.
- Nourish your body properly—for physiological and psychological health.

In summary, healthy lifestyle changes affect your entire makeup—the body, soul, and spirit. As you continue to commit yourself to building a body for victory, the principles we have discussed will start making sense as you experience them for yourself.

Now it's time to look at a few more customized floor plans. These plans will give you a variety of ideas for custom building your "dream house." In your overall plan for building a healthy body, you cannot ignore or exclude these needed plans for exercise!

CHAPTER 8
Building Phase Four: Prepping for Exercise

Having reached this point in the book, you have had the opportunity to review various planning phases for building your body. Each phase provides several components that can play a unique role in completing a customized building plan that is best suited to meet your specific needs.

In these next two building phases, I will provide for your review variations of plans regarding the vital element of exercise for building your healthy body. Before beginning actual exercise programs, it will be important to complete this phase: "Prepping for Exercise." The secret to successfully making regular exercise a daily part of your life is to learn the principles for managing it mentally one day at a time.

In the next chapter, phase five will give you several exercise programs from which to choose, which will be absolutely imperative for making any building package complete. Because I am a professional custom body redesigner, I have compiled these exercises so that you can choose to implement any or all of the exercise programs and know they will be suitable for you. The variety I offer gives you the options to mix it up, try some different approaches for redesigning your body, and avoid mental boredom in the process.

PREPARING TO SUCCEED IN EXERCISE

First, however, it will be very important that you understand that your success in phase five depends on your understanding of the principles and preparation needed for successful exercise. I have witnessed many people who make an attempt to begin exercising. Maybe you are one of those who, around the beginning of a new year, make a resolution to attempt to add exercise to your daily life. That's usually when sedentary, overweight, or unhealthy people have had enough with their condition and plan to do something about it. Cheers and blessings for them!

Building your body and health is a work in progress and, like building a house, requires that you take one brick at a time.

Unfortunately, instead of inching their way into an exercise program to get accustomed to this new way of living, they dive in head first and, in four to six painful, blister-forming weeks, hit the wall and are through with it. Their enthusiasm and intentions were high, but they unintentionally joined the drop-out club because they did not use a sensible approach. As a result, they never experience the huge array of benefits that regular exercise would have provided. To avoid dropping out, consider a sensible program one day at a time, and stay focused on your long-term goals. Then you will be able to enjoy the short-term results in the process, while avoiding overkill. Building your body and health is a work in progress and, like building a house, requires that you take one *brick* at a time.

I do not want you to become an "exercise dropout." To avoid this common catastrophe, consider the following suggestions for making exercise a regular part of your lifestyle. I call these considerations for making exercise fit into your zone, not you fitting into an exercise zone. For example, you need to consider several factors crucial to success before you put on your jogging shoes and head for the streets. These include the current state of your health, your history of exercise, your schedule, your physical structure or genetic needs or specifications, as well as your personal goals. I will help you with these elements in our following discussion, as well as the importance of understanding basic muscle function. You also need to understand what your body experiences in exercise so you can appreciate what you see happening when you look in the mirror for changes. Before giving you plans to choose from, let's take a quick look at these areas so that you will be prepared for the exercise programs.

EXERCISE QUESTIONNAIRE

If you were to ask me to design a custom body redesigning package for you, the first thing I would have you do is fill out a questionnaire. I would need to know some personal history, like the status of your current health, and if you have had any major surgeries or injuries. I would ask you about your exercise background, what you consider your physical limitations, if you take medications, and what is your availability. How much time are you willing to commit to your program? I would do a dietary analysis to find out what type of eater you are. I would need to know your blood type. I would also do a body analysis profile to determine your body genetics so you would have a specialized or customized exercise program geared for your specific body genetics.

If you were planning to build your own house, you would

certainly conduct the same kind of detailed analysis I am doing in preparing a redesigning program for your body before making such a huge investment. Please consider the building of your body an even larger investment, because unlike a house, you only get one body for life. I also would recommend that you see your physician before getting started, especially if you are a female over thirty-five years old or a male over forty years old. It's a good idea to get checked out before you get started. So make an appointment with your physician before you use any of the programs in this book.

The questionnaires on pages 148–152 are examples of the kind of information you need to consider before beginning an exercise program.

Availability—time

After supplying the initial questionnaire and background data, you and I would discuss your availability for exercising. We would evaluate your schedule. This is one of the most important areas of your fitness profiling. It is also the number one excuse that most people use to justify their lack of exercise. Unfortunately, trying to fit thirty extra minutes into your day for exercise is almost impossible, but you must fit it in! If you make the proper lifestyle adjustments, you will find the time. We all do!

Generally, all of us live very busy lives, myself included. That is why it is necessary to analyze the way we use our time and make the necessary adjustments to include daily exercise. Our days are filled with everything from carting the kids off to school in the morning to picking them up in the evening when they finish their after-school programs. In between, there is your job, with all the extra hours you can grab so you can make ends meet.

Or perhaps you are involved in corporate America, with its many demands—such as deadlines, traveling, or after-hours meetings. Then, of course, you have to squeeze in some recreation, social gatherings, church functions, and maybe a movie or two around your work, if you have time. If you are married and have family, you have to make some quality time for your spouse and children. Only then can you consider some quality time for yourself. Sound familiar? It probably does because most Americans are way too busy, overstressed, and consequently too unhealthy to enjoy their life to the fullest.

If what I described above sounds a little like your life, it is likely that you are living your life on a treadmill, and you have probably entered the *overload zone.* To know if your lifestyle is overloaded with the demands of life, take a minute to answer the questions in my Overload Zone chart below. This is a good exercise for doing some important inventory that won't require any physical exertion.

✓ YES	✓ NO	**ARE YOU IN THE OVERLOAD ZONE?**	
		1.	Do you make time for personal prayer with God?
		2.	Do you take time to look at His creation around you?
		3.	Do you have sufficient spiritual strength?
		4.	Do you spend enough quality time with your spouse?
		5.	Do you work at fine-tuning your marriage relationship?
		6.	Do you spend quality time with your children/ teenagers?
		7.	Do you connect with their needs by listening?
		8.	Do you sit down and relax to eat?
		9.	Do you consider what you eat: taste, quality, and quantity?
		10.	Do you have time in your daily schedule for exercise?

✓ YES	✓ NO	ARE YOU IN THE OVERLOAD ZONE?
		11. Do you have energy for exercising?
		12. Do you feel you are experiencing vibrant health?
		13. Do you have good resistance to colds?
		14. Do you find yourself relaxed when driving your car?
		15. Do you consider your life free from complaining?
		16. Do you say hello to passersby?
		17. Do you focus your thoughts on positive things?
		18. Do you set goals?
		19. Do you reach your goals?
		20. Do you prioritize your life?

If you answered *no* to at least three of these questions, you may want to consider doing some lifestyle fine-tuning. If you answered *no* to four to six questions, it's time for minor lifestyle overhaul. If you answered *no* to seven or more questions, your lifestyle is on a collision course, and you are in need of a major lifestyle overhaul—now!

God has designed the human body very uniquely to withstand hard work and endure many difficulties, but it requires proper maintenance. Your body needs a balance of exercise, diet, nutrition, work, and relaxation, besides emotional and spiritual conditioning and healthy human relationships. When any of these areas are lacking, you are actually limiting yourself to a life that is less than desirable.

Living "on the edge" all the time, without a minute to spare, is abusive to your being, causing your life to become unbalanced. In reality, you are setting yourself up for failure in many areas of your life. If you are there now, it is time to make the necessary changes to refocus your energy. Count the cost. What are the most important things in your life? Make a list of priorities. Adjust your schedule, and remember that satisfaction in life is all about relationships. Consider the following priority list as you attempt to adjust your lifestyle, bringing it into an acceptable balance.

PRIORITY LIST

Your relationship and:

1. God
2. Spouse
3. Family
4. Vocation
5. Church
6. Health—personal, financial, emotional
7. Outside relationships, friends, business

When you realize you are forfeiting some valid areas of your life, remember the warning words of the apostle Paul: "Be not deceived; God is not mocked: for whatsoever a man soweth, that shall he also reap" (Gal. 6:7). Simply put, if we sow a lack of relationship, we will reap a lack of relationship. I think you are getting the picture of the importance of prepping yourself before lunging into your bodybuilding program. It is wise to live one day at a time.

THE PHYSIOLOGY OF MUSCLE RESPONSE

To further prepare you for adding regular exercise into your lifestyle, a better understanding of how your muscles respond when you use them in a continuous motion will be helpful. Whether it's for a brief activity, like lifting a cup of coffee to your mouth, or thirty minutes of constant exercise, knowing how your muscles respond helps you appreciate the awesome way your body was created. It will also help you understand why you need to begin your new exercise program slowly instead of jumping into it in a way that creates overkill. Your muscles may not be conditioned to be used with such intensity, so overloading them too quickly is not what they need.

Allow me to take you on a very basic neurological/muscle response journey to show you what takes place when you decide to activate your muscles to perform a physical activity. I promise not to lose you in the intricacies of muscle physiology. Just let me share a couple of illustrations that will simplify this complex process for you.

Remember our discussion of the electrical currents your brain sends throughout your body. There are nerve endings that also attach to your muscles, which receive electrical messages traveling through your spinal cord from the brain. These messages call your muscles into action or response. This neurological response is responsible for the tasks your muscles perform. Also known as muscle recruitment, your muscles are electrically stimulated to contract and perform a particular action. For example, when you decide to take a sip of coffee, the action all starts in your brain. Your brain sends a neurological message to your arm to lift the 8-ounce cup of coffee from the table to your mouth.

Though the task is so simple a child can perform it, lifting that cup to your mouth will actually require several different muscle groups to join in the performance. The major muscles involved are your forearm and biceps muscles, along with the deltoid (shoulder) muscles. Of course, the muscles in your hand also assist the action. All of the muscles are electrically stimulated in the brain and activated to perform their individual tasks in a simultaneous, continuous response pattern, which results in bringing the cup to your mouth.

It is equally fascinating to observe that, in its journey from the table to your mouth, the cup did not hit your nose or forehead. It went directly to your lips. Though the brain commands the body (in this case, your arm) to perform the task, your muscles themselves wouldn't know if the object was a coffee cup, dumbbell, or doughnut. Without the brain giving the commands, electrically stimulating each muscle involved, you could never move your arm from the table. It all begins with the decision to do something and then allowing the neurological electrical impulses to do their thing. The process works from within to complete the external task.

> *All of the muscles are electrically stimulated in the brain and activated to perform their individual tasks in a simultaneous, continuous response pattern.*

You may be aware that in the structure of a muscle, there are thousands of muscle fibers that make up each particular muscle or muscle group. The muscle groups involved in lifting the coffee cup experienced hundreds, or perhaps thousands, of muscle fibers being stimulated. Consider how many times you perform that action to finish drinking that cup of coffee. That represents quite a bit of muscular activity for such a small task. By the way, that simple physical activity required energy (though a very slight amount), which is measured in calories burned. All this muscle fiber stimulation or recruitment causes movement, which in turn burns calories.

The more muscle contractions performed, the more calories burned. By continually recruiting muscle fiber, you eventually develop more muscle and greater strength. All it requires is additional repetitions and additional weight or resistance. Using our example, you would progress from handling an 8-ounce cup of coffee to a 14-ounce cup, and increase the number of trips to your mouth. The end result? Not only will you be drinking more coffee, but you will also be developing more muscles in the process. But let's lift a dumbbell instead!

Repetition is also needed to perfect the motion from the table to your mouth. By adding repetitious action, not only are you burning more calories, but you also improve your proficiency of lifting the cup to your mouth. The ability to improve the control of your movements enhances your motor skills. In this illustration, that means you will become one heck of a coffee drinker with practice. In essence, that's how a person improves their performance in sports, in music, and even in driving a car. Improved motor skills are developed by continuous neurological/physical motion or repetitions.

A second illustration regarding muscle responses involves watching an infant develop his muscles and motor skills, which allow him to lift an object to his mouth. Of course, regardless of what the object is, it is headed for the mouth. But if you have watched this process in a baby's life, you know that the journey to the mouth is not always in a straight line. In fact, until the muscles are strengthened and developed so they can contract more forcefully, along with the necessary development of motor skills, that object he holds will go through a continual succession of awkward motions before it reaches its final destination—the infant's mouth.

As the infant "practices" these movements daily, he starts developing those muscles and motor skills required so that the object can get to his mouth in a much more controlled, decisive way. This developmental process of muscle strength and motor skills continues to improve, allowing the infant to hold his bottle and, eventually, to graduate to a "sippy" cup. Finally, in the child's normal development process, he progresses enough in strength and motor skills to be trusted with an open-mouth cup. These muscles have done many repetitions for the development of the motor skills required for this task.

Remember that every motor skill begins in your brain both

electrically and mentally. Once that child grows into an adult, lifting that cup of coffee to his mouth is no problem because the muscles are conditioned and the motor skills have become very proficient from repeated use.

Applying these principles to your exercise program, your muscles may not be conditioned or strengthened for an advanced program. If you have been living a sedentary life-style on the couch or otherwise have taken a long reprieve from physical exercise, your muscles are not ready for a major blast of an intense exercise routine. That's why I suggest when you begin to exercise, take it one day at a time. Exercising your entire body involves many more muscles and moving body parts than lifting a cup of coffee to your mouth, though the basic principle for success is the same. I refer to this approach as *progressive fitness training.*

As I begin to present different strategies for exercise, please consider the importance of our discussion for initial prepara-tion mentally and physically before you begin. Then you will be ready to choose from the variety of approaches to exercise for different lifestyle situations, regarding where and when to exer-cise and the type of equipment you should consider using.

HEALTH QUESTIONNAIRE

The following questions/answers will help us be more accurate in designing your program.

Are you planning to exercise at home?   ☐ yes ☐ no

If *yes*, please describe the type of equipment that you will be using (brand name, multistation machine, free weights, rowing machine, stationary bike, etc.). Please include photos if possible.

_____

_____

_____

_____

Do you need assistance in selecting equipment for your home?

☐ yes ☐ no

If *yes*, please give the name, address, phone number, and person to contact.

_____

_____

_____

_____

Please write a paragraph (25–50 words) on why you would like to improve your health and physical appearance.

_____

_____

_____

_____

_____

_____

_____

HEALTH HISTORY FORM

Name: _____   Date: _____

Sex: Male ____Female ____

Physician Name: _____

Address: _____

_____

Phone number: _____

What is your blood type? ☐ A ☐ B ☐ AB ☐ O ☐ Don't know

Are you taking medications or drugs? _____ If yes, please list:

_____   _____

_____   _____

Does your physician know that you are planning to participate in this exercise program? _____

Please describe your current exercise program, if any.

_____

_____

Do you now have, or have you had in the past: *(please check)*	YES	NO
1. History of heart problems, chest pain, or stroke?	☐	☐
2. Increased blood pressure?	☐	☐
3. Any chronic illness or condition?	☐	☐
4. Difficulty with physical exercise?	☐	☐
5. Advice from the doctor not to exercise?	☐	☐
6. Pregnancy (now or within last three months)?	☐	☐
7. Recent surgery (within past twelve months)?	☐	☐
8. History of breathing or lung problems?	☐	☐
9. Muscle, joint, or back disorder, or any previous injury still affecting you?	☐	☐
10. Cigarette smoking habit?	☐	☐
11. Thyroid or diabetes condition?	☐	☐
12. Obesity (more than 20% over ideal body weight)?	☐	☐
13. Increased blood cholesterol?	☐	☐
14. History of heart problems in immediate family?	☐	☐
15. Hernia or any condition that may be aggravated by lifting weights?	☐	☐

If you answered *yes* to any of the above questions, please explain:

_____

_____

_____

_____

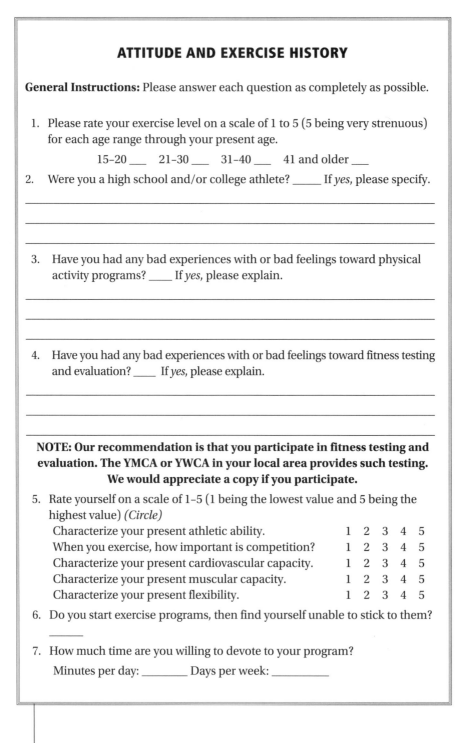

ATTITUDE AND EXERCISE HISTORY

General Instructions: Please answer each question as completely as possible.

1. Please rate your exercise level on a scale of 1 to 5 (5 being very strenuous) for each age range through your present age.

    15–20 ___   21–30 ___   31–40 ___   41 and older ___

2. Were you a high school and/or college athlete? _____ If *yes*, please specify.

    _____

    _____

    _____

3. Have you had any bad experiences with or bad feelings toward physical activity programs? ____ If *yes*, please explain.

    _____

    _____

    _____

4. Have you had any bad experiences with or bad feelings toward fitness testing and evaluation? ____ If *yes*, please explain.

    _____

    _____

    _____

NOTE: Our recommendation is that you participate in fitness testing and evaluation. The YMCA or YWCA in your local area provides such testing. We would appreciate a copy if you participate.

5. Rate yourself on a scale of 1–5 (1 being the lowest value and 5 being the highest value) *(Circle)*

Characterize your present athletic ability.	1 2 3 4 5
When you exercise, how important is competition?	1 2 3 4 5
Characterize your present cardiovascular capacity.	1 2 3 4 5
Characterize your present muscular capacity.	1 2 3 4 5
Characterize your present flexibility.	1 2 3 4 5

6. Do you start exercise programs, then find yourself unable to stick to them?

    _____

7. How much time are you willing to devote to your program?

    Minutes per day: _____ Days per week: _____

8. Are you currently involved in regular endurance-type exercise? _____ If *yes*, please specify the type of exercise, minutes per day, and days per week:

    Type: _____

    Minutes per day: _____ Hours per week: _____

    Circle the level of exertion of your exercise program:
    A. Light   B. Fairly light   C. Somewhat hard   D. Hard

9. How long have you been exercising regularly?
    Months: _____ Years: _____

10. What other sport, exercise, or recreational activity have you participated in during...
    the past 6 months? _____
    the past 5 years? _____

11. Can you exercise during your work day? _____

12. If you answered *yes* to question 11, would the exercise program interfere with your job? _____

13. If you answered *yes* to question 11, would the exercise program benefit your job? _____

14. What types of exercise interest you?

Walking ___	Stationary biking ___	Jogging ___
Rowing ___	Strength training ___	Cycling ___
Tennis ___	Dance exercise ___	Golfing ___
Stretching ___	Other aerobic (specify) _____	

15. Rate your goals in undertaking exercise. What do you want exercise to do for you? Rate yourself from 1 to 10, with 1 being extremely important, 5 being somewhat important, and 10 being not important.
    ____ A. Improve cardiovascular fitness
    ____ B. Body-fat weight loss
    ____ C. Redesign or tone body
    ____ D. Improve performance for a specific sport
    ____ E. Improve moods and ability to cope with stress
    ____ F. Improve flexibility
    ____ G. Increase strength
    ____ H. Increase energy level
    ____ I. Feel better
    ____ J. Enjoyment
    ____ K. Other _____

16. If applicable, how many pounds would you like to gain or lose?
    Gain _____ pounds   Lose _____ pounds

DIETARY ANALYSIS

Please list ALL the FOODS, LIQUIDS, and their AMOUNTS consumed for the last three days.

Day 1   Breakfast   _____

          Midmorning   _____

          Lunch   _____

          Midafternoon   _____

          Dinner   _____

Day 2   Breakfast   _____

          Midmorning   _____

          Lunch   _____

          Midafternoon   _____

          Dinner   _____

Day 3   Breakfast   _____

          Midmorning   _____

          Lunch   _____

          Midafternoon   _____

          Dinner   _____

NOTE: Remember to include *all* the cookies, slices of pizza, cans of soda, etc. If you take nutritional supplements, please list them:

_____

_____

_____

CHAPTER 9

Building Phase Five: Choosing Your Exercise Program

I have divided the following exercise floor plans into seven different categories, which gives flexibility for different lifestyles and preferences. They may all be incorporated into your lifestyle at your convenience, or you may choose one to help you reach your goal of building a body for victory. Each will give you greater understanding of your body's need for movement, stretching, and strengthening, as well as helping to reshape and redesign its weaknesses into strengths.

EXERCISE FLOOR PLAN #1: UNDERSTANDING YOUR BODY TYPE

The key to success in getting the results you want from exercise starts with knowing your body type. Each body type requires a different exercise approach or methodology for reaching its genetic potential. Some types gain weight very easily; other types would have to eat all day to gain weight. Some require very little effort to get great results, while others have to work zealously to see fewer results. There are body types who carry their unwanted weight in the upper body area, and others who gain weight in the hips and thighs. Considering your particular body type will help you choose the exercise program most effective for your needs.

Genetic metabolic body type

To give you an overview of basic body types, let me explain briefly two aspects of importance: your body's genetic *metabolic* abilities and your genetic body *structure*. First, you will need to identify your body type regarding your genetic metabolic abilities, categorized as ectomorph, endomorph, and mesomorph.

Ectomorph

The ectomorph body type has a light frame, which makes it very easy for you to over-train. If you are female, you are often referred to as being *petite*. Ectomorph men are usually tall and underweight for their height. Both typically have a difficult time gaining weight because of their fast metabolism, which makes them the envy of all overweight people. They can usually eat as much as they want without gaining weight.

If you inadvertently over-train, you will have a tendency to tap into your caloric reserves for muscle recovery and growth. To avoid this, try to keep your work intensity high but the duration short. Rest longer in between sets, and don't do many repetitions per exercise. Ideally, you should perform one exercise for every major muscle group. Perform three sets of six to eight repetitions (reps) per major muscle group for the upper body and three sets of ten reps for the major muscle groups for the lower body twice a week. Safely use as much resistance or weight as you can, making sure you stay within the set/rep margins, which are determined by not being able to perform another repetition.

Endomorph

The endomorph body type has a heavy frame and usually

gains weight easily. As an endomorph body type, I seem to be able to gain weight simply by walking past a table filled with food. Because our metabolism is typically sluggish, we need to maintain a physically active lifestyle and avoid overeating .

Workouts for the endomorph are opposite to those of the ectomorph. You should consider performing up to eight to ten sets of twelve to fifteen repetitions for each major muscle group, including both the upper and lower torso. Two exercises would be sufficient per major muscle group. You also need to include plenty of cardiovascular workouts along with your body redesigning workouts if you want to lower your body fat percentage. Exercising every day wouldn't be too much until you reach your desired goal.

Mesomorph

The blessing of the mesomorph is that you have been graced with the more classic, symmetrical physique to begin with. Your body looks like you exercise all the time, even if you never have. You are the envy of those who work out in the gyms every day to improve their physiques, often exhausting themselves to see minimal results, while you are able to do very little and enjoy maximum improvement.

Though your metabolism responds well to most foods, you will still profit by eating according to your blood type. You alone have a natural balance between the upper and lower torsos, in contrast to the other two morph-types. Practically any method of exercise will work for you, so why not try some of the routines I have designed in the book if you haven't tried them before. (For more information on body types, see my books *Seven Pillars of Health* and *Bloodtypes, Bodytypes and You.*)

Genetic body-type structure

The second categorization of body types involves your genetic structure, which determines your predisposed fat deposits. There are three basic genetic body types, which I began to classify over fifteen years ago as *pear, apple,* and *banana.* For each unique body shape, based on predisposed fat deposits, different exercise approaches are required. These are not difficult to determine. You may have already targeted your body shape according to these three fruits. (Please see Appendix D for troubleshooting characteristics of each body-type structure.) Visit my Web site, www.bodyredesigning.com, to obtain a video or DVD workout for each body-type structure.

EXERCISE FLOOR PLAN #2: TRAIN 'EM, THEN STRETCH 'EM

There are several reasons for stretching your muscles. The primary reason is to create more range of motion (ROM) for your joints. Creating greater ROM is a key preventative exercise for healthy joints, soft tissues, and adjacent muscle groups. The greater the ROM, the greater the flexibility of the joint. The greater the flexibility of the joint, the better will be your joint response necessary for performance in every sport, as well as general everyday tasks such as getting off the couch.

By creating more ROM through gentle stretching, you lessen the likelihood for injury to the joints by releasing the body's natural joint fluid: synovial fluid. This fluid acts as a lubricant and a seal around the opposed joint surfaces. By keeping the joints oiled with nature's joint fluid through stretching, you will also experience less pain because of enhanced sliding of the joints across these surfaces.

Keep in mind that surrounding the joints are soft connective tissue or ligaments that attach bone to bone. They are like rubber bands that are very susceptible to overstress and strain, mainly due to lack of exercise. Stretching is also vitally important for the tendons, which are the connective tissues that connect bones to muscles.

Replacing the "old school" routine

For years exercise gurus have told you to "stretch out" before beginning your workout or sports activity. However, that is now considered the "old school" approach to stretching, which is outdated. Now we understand that stretching should be done *after* the muscles have been warmed up—not before. As a jogger, you may be accustomed to stretching out by leaning against telephone poles, stop signs, or even stretching your calves off the edge of a street curb before beginning your jogging routine. Of course, it is vitally important to stretch before intensive exercise such as jogging, because stretching helps elongate the muscles and create blood flow. However, your muscles stretch better after they are warmed up.

If you are planning to jog, for example, then I would suggest that you walk for several blocks or laps around a track for warming up the muscles. At that point, if you feel that the muscles and joints are warm, you can stop to stretch. After a short stretching period (two to four minutes), you can start jogging. After you are finished jogging, stretch again for two to four minutes.

The most advantageous method of stretching you can do is called *static stretching*. This gentle and slow method of stretching will prevent potential injury from overstretching, which is commonly associated with *ballistic stretching*. Ballistic stretching is a more explosive bouncing of the muscles rather than a slow, gentle stretch.

Here is an example of some basic static stretching suggestions you might want to incorporate on a regular basis before a physical event and/or for getting maximum muscle response from your training program:

1. Pre-warming the muscle(s) before a leg workout. For example, warm up before doing leg extensions on the leg extension machine.

A very simple way to warm up the thighs, hips/buttocks muscles, and knees is to perform squats with a chair or bench. Just as you would sit and then stand from a chair, do that simple action for ten, fifteen, or twenty repetitions. This will thoroughly pump blood into those muscles for warmth. Now, you are ready to perform any leg exercise.

After you perform a particular leg exercise, take a minute to stretch each thigh muscle. From a standing position, bend one leg back and reach behind your back and grab the toes. Standing erect, gently pull the foot as high as you can behind you until you feel the knee joint and thigh muscles get comfortably stretched—not painfully tight. Then hold for approximately thirty seconds and release. Perform this on the other leg also.

Of course, you can apply a stretching phase to every muscle group/joint that you are training or are using in an event.

2. Use the static stretch technique after every set of exercises you do to improve the blood flow in the muscle group being trained and stretch the fascia tissue.

3. Drink plenty of water (alkaline preferred) to flush out toxins and acid buildup.

After every training session or sports event, you are going to experience some muscle soreness and possibly joint pain. That is your body's way of letting you know you just passed your present condition and crossed beyond your pain barrier. The muscles might feel tight, but since they are trained muscles, they will stretch out more easily than muscles that are not used. Do the preventative things you should do like stretching daily, and enjoy enhanced performance and maximum recovery.

EXERCISE FLOOR PLAN #3:
GRAVITATIONAL TRAINING

I realize there is a price to pay for getting into shape. I am not just referring to the attitudinal and motivational adjustments required to begin, which give us the willingness to make changes. There is also a dollar value required for most methods of exercise training. Whether it is a membership at a health club/gym, hiring a personal trainer, or buying your own equipment, there is a price tag attached. When this cost becomes prohibitive, it can definitely dampen your plans for building a body for victory.

So, I have designed an exercise plan for you that doesn't require you to spend dollars you don't have. I call it *gravitational training*. As long as God allows the force of gravity to pull everything to the center of the earth, we can get real creative in using that force to our advantage. This very effective and challenging workout program uses gravity as your means for resistance.

The evolution of weightlifting began during the 1930s and 1940s when strongmen performed "the one-arm clean and jerk" and the handlebar mustache separated the men from the boys. Men would prove their strength by bending steel bars with their bare hands, twisting horseshoes for fun, or even humoring themselves with a contest of tearing telephone books in two. It seems that during this time the sport of heavy weight lifting and bodybuilding evolved.

Today, great feats of strength are still being performed, not just by men with handlebar mustaches, but by both men *and* women of strength. My good friends Ray Clark and Jannet Abraham Clark travel all over the country and internationally with a message about making positive choices, demonstrating their message through feats of strength. As they hold the attention of thousands of young people (and adults) with their amazing strength abilities, they also take the opportunity to make a transition from physical strength to spiritual strength. Their message is loud and clear. What a tremendous way to use their body sizes and strength for the good.[1]

> *Today, great feats of strength are still being performed by both men and women of strength.*

As time passed, the sport became more sophisticated, and strength building with its extravagant equipment began to take center stage. Equipment today has evolved into something beyond the imaginations of those yesteryear muscle men. Today we have spring-loaded, cam-driven, isotonic, isometric, and isolation machines; chrome barbell and dumbbell sets with adjustable ratchets; incline/decline and flat benches; chrome-plated, multistation units; bikes; treadmills; and elliptical and stair climbers. The costs for using or owning this equipment has skyrocketed. What used to cost fifteen dollars a month for membership in a black iron gym costs the same as a car payment today. To outfit a decent home gym with all the equipment you need would require you to get another part-time job.

Since not everyone can afford the luxury of a gym membership or to equip their own home gym, my gravitational training program is designed as an effective workout that you can do at home, at the office, in your hotel room, or other suitable places. There is no extra charge for equipment, because there is no equipment needed. Choose it as your main exercise program, or use it when you cannot access other equipment.

Push-ups for upper body: chest, arms, shoulders

Perform the standard push-up from your knees. Start in the up position with the arms locked and palms and toes (knees) on the floor. Lower body until the chest touches the floor, then return to the starting position. Perform three sets of ten repetitions (reps) for each position. One set includes the following three positions: wider-than-shoulder hand spacing, shoulder-width hand spacing, and narrow hand spacing with both thumbs touching. Do not rest until all three positions are completed.

Door pull-ups for back, arms, forearms

Use the door in your room. Grab the door handles on both sides of the door while facing the opened door. Brace your feet at the bottom of the door, lean back while lowering your buttocks to the floor. Pull yourself back to the standing position; repeat for twelve reps. Do three sets of twelve reps.

Crunches for abdominal muscles

Lie on the floor. Put your lower legs (calves) on a chair or couch or other furniture of that height to support your legs. Bend your legs to form a 90-degree angle between your legs and your torso. Roll your head and shoulders up approximately 4 to 5 inches off the floor and crunch, tightening the abdominal muscles. Hold that position for ten seconds. Return to the start position and repeat for twenty reps. Do four sets of twenty reps.

Door squats for lower body: legs

Again, use the door in your room. Grab both door handles while facing the opened door. Keep your feet parallel with arms and back straight. Lean back and squat down so your thigh muscles are in a parallel position to the floor. Return to the start position. *Do not lock your knees* when standing. Do four sets of twenty reps.

Well, there it is—a complete body workout with no monetary investment. I dare you to give this a real go, being grateful it didn't cost you a dime for equipment. After doing this routine three times a week for two weeks, challenge yourself to do it five times a week. I promise that you will shock your body into a new level of fitness.

EXERCISE FLOOR PLAN #4:
TOTAL BODY WORKOUT IN YOUR HOME GYM

Having your own home gym is my idea of the way to fly. Obviously, everyone cannot own a $25,000 state-of-the-art home gymnasium. If you are one of those privileged few who can, I would like to know it and come over for a workout. For most people, it is important to keep it simple and practical yet efficient. Remember, it's how you use the tool that makes the difference, not necessarily the tool itself.

Keeping your home gym affordable by simply equipping it with the bare essentials is adequate to help you build a body for victory. For that purpose, you should start with a run of dumbbells from 5 pounds to 30 pounds, and a flat bench or one that is adjustable for inclined movements. Many people select a multiple station exercise unit that has nearly everything you need.

For cardiovascular exercise, you would want a treadmill, stationary bike, or any cardiovascular piece of equipment that you will enjoy most. If you prefer to walk or run outside, you can save a few bucks.

Then, of course, you can add the big boys—an Olympic weight set and barbells—as part of your equipment as well. Add a couple of mirrors and a CD player, and you are in business. Your gym should be equipped with these basics so you can train your total body.

A basic total body workout should consist of exercising all the major muscle groups three days a week and, on your "off" days, adding some cardiovascular work. This combination works well together, though I don't recommend that you do more than twenty minutes of cardiovascular training at a time.

Here's a basic routine to follow that incorporates all the major muscle groups. This is not a customized program. Later in this section, I'll address a genetically compatible workout for your body type; for now, this routine is "middle of the road."

Warmup

Just do enough movement to get some blood circulation and muscle/joint warming. Try ten to fifteen minutes on your cardio equipment. If you include stretching in your workout, do it after you are through training, or at least thoroughly warmed up.

Most fitness equipment comes with a chart or video that illustrates each exercise, cardiovascular heart training zones, and many other things. If it doesn't, go to your local sporting goods store and ask for instructions for basic exercises, which are usually readily available.

Upper body

If you are a novice or not acquainted with the exercises that are listed, you may want to jot them down or take this book with you to your local YMCA or fitness club. Ask an instructor or personal trainer to assist you in getting familiar with the exercises and performance know-how.

When choosing the right amount of weight, apply this rule: If the weight is too heavy to complete a set, lower the amount of weight. If at the end of a set, you could continue more reps with ease, increase the weight. If by the end of the set, it is a little challenging, but fairly easy to complete that last rep, the weight is just right. You want to feel a little burn without straining or overstressing your muscles.

A complete workout for the upper body will include the following:

- Chest: Chest press with machine or dumbbells. Perform four sets of twelve reps.
- Back: Pull-downs with machine. Do four sets of twelve reps.
- Shoulders: Seated overhead presses with dumbbells or machine. Do four sets of twelve reps.

- Biceps: Standing or seated curls with dumbbells. Do four sets of twelve reps.
- Triceps: Triceps press-down with machine. Do four sets of twelve reps.

Lower body

- Thighs/buttocks/hamstrings: Lunges with or without dumbbells. Do four sets of fifteen reps.
- Thighs: Leg extensions with machine. Do four sets of fifteen to twenty reps.
- Calves: Calf raises on a step. Do four sets of twenty reps.
- Abdominal: Crunches. Do four sets of twenty-five reps.

The sets and reps listed above are the ideal goal for your total body workout. As I have emphasized throughout, you need to start into your exercise program gradually. Perform one or two sets per exercise when you start, then work your way up to performing all of the sets and reps. Listen to what your body says. Don't overdo it. If you feel light-headed or dizzy, stop the workout. Your goal is to make progress over time, not all in one day.

EXERCISE FLOOR PLAN #5: SPECIALIZED TRAINING

Total body training is essential for developing overall strength and body conditioning. For most people, just getting to do a total body workout on a regular basis three times a week is quite an accomplishment in itself. One can see very good improvement in their overall health, energy levels, stamina, and physique by staying with it. To take fitness to another level for specific purposes, however, requires specialized training.

For example, some reasons to specialize can be to enhance sports and athletic performance, to create a needed balance in the physique or body symmetry, to gain larger size and shape, and to reduce size as well. To add to the exercise plans for building a body for victory, here are specialized training programs for you to review.

The legs are king.

This specialized exercise workout for legs is appropriate for men and women, but especially for those with an "apple" body type, which is characterized partly by under-sized legs and buttocks. The goal of the workout is to build leg size, balance leg development, and enhance sports performance, if desired.

To decide if this workout will be beneficial for you, try to answer the question: "Are your tires flat?" In all my travels to present health and fitness programs, I have had many kinds of questions directed to me regarding which muscle or muscle groups are most important to train. Is there a single muscle group that can be considered "king"? For the record, every muscle group is important, and none should be neglected. However, to answer the question whether or not one muscle group could be rated above the others, in my estimation, it would be the leg muscles.

Let me defend that statement with the following analogy. Let's say your car has been in need of a tune-up for quite some time; you have neglected your car in much the same way we often neglect our health. So you decide to take your car down to the mechanic to get it fine-tuned, or, if you are the fix-it-up-yourself kind of person, you do it yourself. After the repairs to your engine are completed, it purrs like a kitten, and everything runs smoothly again. The car is in perfect condition for the highway. You decide to take it for a drive and are cruising along on the interstate when, suddenly, you feel the car begin to swerve, sort of steering erratically, and then you hear the flap, flap, flapping sound. It doesn't take long to realize you have a flat tire!

At this point it doesn't matter if you have a 400-cubic-inch engine with double turbo and all the power under the hood that one car can carry. Your tire is flat, and your ride lurches to a complete standstill. Now you have a couple of options: you can continue driving on the flat (we all know how far that will get you), or you can fix the problem by replacing the flat tire with a new solid tire.

It is not difficult to apply this analogy to your body's performance and to your legs specifically. You can be diligently following excellent plans for taking care of your health, like supplementing with proper nutrients, eating according to your blood type, and exercising regularly. But if you are not "hitting" those legs, you will never experience satisfactory results in performance for sports, for muscle development, for endurance, or for a super capacity to burn fat. To apply this reality to the building analogy, you must consider your legs as the pillars that support your superstructure—God's temple.

If you want to experience the ultimate success from your training experience, you must incorporate into your other programs at least an equal effort in building leg strength. Training your legs will enhance your cardiovascular conditioning (heart) and improve your capacity for oxygen uptake (VO2 max) (lungs) as well. Because your legs represent your largest muscle groups, they demand more oxygen and blood to be pumped into them. For that reason, working the legs places a great demand on the heart and lungs, making this workout more intense. It is also the reason many people neglect giving their leg workout the proper intensity needed to be effective.

Anyone who has ever performed deep knee bends or squats can attest to the intense burning feeling created, not only in the legs, but also in their lungs. If you don't believe me, just perform one set of fifty deep knee bends or squats to a chair or bench. Then call me after the paramedics have resuscitated you and tell me how your lungs are feeling and how weak your legs feel. (Please don't try this. I am just making a point.) In short, it is a true statement that the legs are king.

Because your thighs are the largest muscle groups in your body, they require more work for total body efficiency than any other muscle groups. While that may seem logical, the fact is that most people spend more time training their arm and chest muscles (the visible muscles groups) than they do training their legs, which is totally opposite to properly training your body for symmetry as well as overall health. Consequently, their physiques are out of balance, and their overall strength and endurance are lagging.

> *You must consider your legs as the pillars that support your superstructure—God's temple.*

Until you have thoroughly trained your legs, you won't be able to appreciate the overall strength and energy you will enjoy when they are well conditioned. A specialized leg routine will deplete your stamina and endurance during the workout, from both the cardiovascular and localized conditioning aspects, making your legs feel like strings of pasta. But as your leg conditioning improves, so will your lung capacity, which will result in a higher level of energy. As a result of the greater strength you will experience when your legs are conditioned, your total body conditioning is benefited, and you reach a higher level of overall fitness. Leg-specializing exercise programs benefit sports performance, day-to-day tasks, job performance, and just about everything else you do. Remember, when those "tires" are flat, so is your overall performance.

AUTHOR'S NOTE: Before continuing, please let me make it very clear that the following suggestion for a specialization leg workout is not meant to be continued indefinitely. You should plan to specialize for *no longer than three months*. Regardless of your current condition, remember to do only what you are capable of doing. Remember to apply the rule mentioned in the upper body workout section when choosing the right amount of weight.

Specialized leg workout

To begin this leg workout, you first want to warm up. Keep in mind that your legs are comprised of several muscle groups that include the quadriceps (teardrop muscles), located above and on both sides of your knees; the hamstrings (rear thigh muscles), located behind the knee and attached to the top of your calves; tying into the *gluteus maximus* (your buttocks); and of course the "glutes" themselves. The glutes are the muscles that provide the power and strength for sports performance, such as running and sprinting, skiing, skating, squatting, almost every sport that requires explosive exhilaration.

When the thighs and buttocks are well trained, they can also be very shapely. It is an interesting fact that in bodybuilding competition, careful training of the legs is imperative to be considered totally balanced and developed to the maximum.

With an understanding of the various muscles involved in your legs, you will want to make sure you *warm up the entire lower body thoroughly* before you begin your leg-training program. To warm up your lower body, perform two sets of deep knee bends to a bench or chair for twenty repetitions. You could also use a stationary bike for five to ten minutes. The following exercises can be performed as your routine for the legs. Remember to select the amount of weight that is challenging for the repetitions and sets per exercise.

Squats with barbell

This is a compound movement, meaning that it involves more than one primary muscle to perform the exercise. Place the bar across your shoulders. Keep a solid upright position with the chest held high. Take a shoulder-width stance, and make sure you keep your head up throughout the movement. (Looking down has a tendency to cause you to tip forward.)

Don't hold your breath; try to breathe naturally. Bend your knees and squat down until the top of the thighs are parallel to the floor; then return to the start position. Your beginning goal is to perform two sets of fifteen to twenty reps without weights. But, remember, start slow and easy.

If you prefer not to use a barbell, you can use a Smith machine or squat machine. This exercise works the quadriceps and buttocks muscles.

Leg presses

This exercise is also a compound movement, usually performed on a 45-degree leg press machine or sled. This exercise doesn't require balance. All you have to do is press the weight until the knees are just about locked and then return slowly. Once you are positioned at the base of the machine and your feet are spaced about shoulder width, lower the weight down as far as you can, making sure your back stays flat against the pads. Push back to starting position and repeat until all the reps are completed. Again, begin with two sets of fifteen to twenty reps, if possible. This exercise also works the quadriceps.

Leg curls

Lie face down or sit upright, depending on the type of leg curl machine you are using. Once positioned properly, bend your knees to curl the pads backward until you reach the maximum distance; then return to the start position, and repeat. This exercise works the hamstring muscles behind the thighs.

Varying the routine

During your three-month leg specialization workout, work your way up to four sets of twenty-five reps for each exercise, using a weight that is challenging. Start with the squats, and end up with the leg curls. For variety the first month, begin doing them in the order listed. After that, mix the order or sequence during the next two months to provide variety and constant stimulation.

For the duration of this specializing period for your legs, discontinue all other thigh/leg movements, and concentrate only on these two compound movements, squats and leg presses, along with leg curls. These will allow you the capacity for pushing more weight, stimulating more muscle for more growth, and taking your total body size and strength to another level. Give it a try, but don't be surprised if those pleated slacks get stretched out a little bit. And remember, your legs are the pillars that support your superstructure—God's temple.

Specialized chest workout

This specialized exercise workout for the chest is appropriate for men and women, but especially for those with a "pear" body type, which is characterized by under-sized pectoral muscles. The goal is to build body symmetry as well as strength for sports and other activities. Pumping up those pecs can be an important contribution to the overall building of a body for victory.

As we discussed, I believe the legs are "king" in prioritizing muscle training, because strong, conditioned legs set the pace for the rest of the body concerning strength and endurance. If I were to categorize which muscle groups have the most appeal, I would say it is the chest muscles (pectorals). They are probably the most popular group of all for muscular training.

For men, the pectoral muscles have always been considered one of the most visible of the Herculean assets. Let's face it; when it comes to filling out those T-shirts, there is nothing like a huge chest to contrast with the rest of the physique. In my travels as a personal fitness coach, I have not only helped hundreds of men but women as well to fill out their chest muscles to balance their physical appearance. Many of the female pageant contestants I have trained for the swimsuit portion of their competitions in the Miss America or Miss USA pageants enhanced their overall appearance with a specialized chest routine.

Years ago, while traveling as corporate fitness and nutrition coach for Planet Hollywood, I spent a couple of weeks in London, England. Besides training one of the owners of Planet Hollywood and many of his Hollywood celebrity friends, I had the unexpected opportunity to train a famous pop vocalist in a specialized chest routine. I was working one evening in the gym at the Dorchester Hotel in London when he came in for a workout with his personal trainer.

As his trainer was putting the pop vocalist through his routine, I observed the workout. I went over and introduced myself to the pop vocalist and asked him what his fitness goals were. He responded that his goal was to build his chest muscles. I realized that the routine he was following was not sufficient to produce a sweat, let alone pump his pecs. I asked him if he would be interested in trying a couple of movements I suggested. Graciously, he let me take him through a "mini" chest workout. We finished the demonstration of the brief chest "stimulator" and went our separate ways. I remained in the gym to finish my workout after he had already hit the showers. I happened to look out into the hallway that led to the showers in time to see my friend trying to stretch his arms backwards to loosen his pectorals. I could tell that he knew he had just experienced the best chest workout of his life by the pained, but elated, expression on his face.

There are two primary muscle groups to consider when building the chest: the pectoral major and the pectoral minor. The secondary muscles that come into play when training the pectorals are the front deltoid muscles (shoulders) and the triceps of the upper arms.

An important part of developing your specialization routine is to determine what exactly your overall chest area needs to make it symmetrical with the rest of your body. Do your pectorals need more width or depth? Or do they need both? Is the upper part of your chest shallow? Once you determine what you need, then you can decide what to do to produce the desired effect. While I cannot give all the possible specializations here, I will get you on track by giving you several exercises that will form a basic foundation for developing your pectoral muscles.

Equipment needed

- Dumbbells—weights that are held in each hand
- Adjustable flat bench—a weight bench that can be set at different angles from flat to inclined
- Pec deck or butterfly machine—a weight machine used for exercising the chest muscles
- Parallel or dip bars—used to raise and lower the body (in a push-up position) by using the arm and chest muscles

I recommend that you use dumbbells for your chest routine instead of a straight bar that many people use. While the straight bar may be great for lifting heavier weights, it limits the range of motion that helps to effectively develop the pectorals. Dumbbells allow you to lower the weight below the level of the chest, which makes them more effective because of the greater range of motion allowed.

An adjustable bench will give you the versatility of working the chest muscles from different angles. Setting your adjustable bench in the flat position will allow you to hit the belly of the muscle (pectoral major). The dumbbell bench press, pressing upward from your chest with a dumbbell in each hand as you lie on your back on the bench, is ideal for this one. The incline bench position will hit the upper chest (the shallow pectoral minors). The trick to the incline is to remember *not* to raise the incline position more than 30 degrees. Most conventional inclined benches are at a 60- to 75-degree angle or more—not good! If the angle is too high, it places most of the workload on the front shoulders and less on the upper chest muscles.

If your home gym or the gym you visit has a pec deck or butterfly machine, incorporate it into your program as well. This exercise will hit the inner pectorals and help fill out the center of the chest. This is considered an isolation exercise as it isolates the targeted muscle without the assistance of the secondary muscles. In women, it develops cleavage.

Performing dips (raising and lowering the entire body) on parallel bars is a great basic exercise for building the chest. It is considered a compound exercise because it involves the triceps/shoulders as well as the chest muscles. If you want most of the workload to go directly to the pectorals, then lean forward while descending and raising up. Try to keep your eyes focused on an object in front on you to maintain this position throughout the movement. This is a tough one because you are lifting your body weight. Some gyms have an apparatus that offsets your body weight by letting you kneel on a weight support platform until you are strong enough to perform dips using your full body weight.

The repetitions and sets should be the basic four sets of twelve to fifteen reps for three workouts a week. Of course, that is your goal, not your starting point. As for the amount of weight to use, that is going to be an individual call. You have selected the proper weight to begin with if you can complete the last rep of the last set with ease. After that, advancing to a heavier increment should also be determined by your ability to complete the last rep of the last set with ease. If you can do more reps than twelve to fifteen, that is an indication to add more weight.

If you want to hit the outside area of the chest to make your chest grow wider, then use a wide-hand spacing. That means if you are using the dumbbells for flat bench presses or inclines, keep the bells further out to the sides. If you want more depth or thicker pectorals, keep the hand spacing closer together. This you can do when doing dumbbell bench presses by keeping your elbows close to your chest as you perform the exercise.

With these basic movements and the appropriate equipment, you should be able to stimulate those pectorals and give your physique that added symmetry and balance. Remember to warm up thoroughly before starting the routine. Take a very light pair of dumbbells (lighter than you use for your actual routine), and perform two sets of twenty repetitions in the dumbbell bench press exercise.

EXERCISE FLOOR PLAN #6:
EXERCISING ON THE ROAD

In our extremely mobile society, many people do a lot of traveling with their job situations, as well as for recreation purposes. A great concern for them is how to maintain their exercise program while they are on the road. Whether you travel for work, pleasure, or vacation, let me give you some things to think about before you have to leave town again.

As your fellow traveler, I can relate to your concerns regarding the need to often improvise a workout program while on the road. Traveling can be very disruptive to your regular workout program, along with being physically draining and stressful as travel often is. That makes it even more important to exercise while on the road. There are some simple solutions to the dilemma of getting a proper workout.

Travel exercise solutions

Perhaps the most simple solution to getting a basic, overall workout while traveling is to follow the basic routine I outlined earlier, which I call gravity training. This routine gives you a great workout without the need for conventional exercise equipment. (See page 159.) To perform these exercises, all you need is for gravity to act as the resistance factor, which, of course, is a no-brainer.

However, because of the demand today for fitness "stations," many hotels and convention centers offer well-equipped facilities for their guests. Before I leave town, I call the hotel where I'm going to stay to see if they have a fitness room and inquire as to the type of amenities the hotel offers. Unfortunately, unless you are staying at a more elaborate hotel, the equipment available in the fitness room is often limited to one or two treadmills, a stationary bike or two, and maybe a knee-destroying step machine. If you are fortunate, there could be a row of dumbbells ascending up to 10 pounds, which can help to keep up your momentum. It is at least more profitable than sitting around all night in your hotel room and channel surfing.

The most important consideration is to maintain your muscle tone and strength in order to prevent muscle atrophy. This is a condition whereby the muscles weaken, losing their tone, strength, and size. You may not be aware that muscle atrophy begins within a twenty-four- to forty-eight-hour period after your last workout. Extended travel without exercising has fitness catastrophe written all over it. In case the hotel fitness room doesn't actually have fitness equipment but does have cardiovascular equipment like bikes or treadmills, at least get your cardiovascular workouts in while staying there. You can also go outside, if the weather and environment permits, and walk or jog.

When I call my hotel and receive the answer that there is no fitness room, I then inquire if there is a local gym located near the hotel. Many times the hotels have arrangements with a local gym to give their guests a pass to use their facilities. If none of these options are available, it is time to get creative.

One solution, other than the basic gravity training that you can easily accommodate, is to carry a flex cord in your bag.

There are many variations of flex cords that you can check out at your local sporting goods store. Generally they come with a foldout sheet with exercise photos to follow or even a workout video. Since they are portable and can be stored in your suitcase or gym bag, taking your flexible "gym equipment" while you travel is a great idea.

Muscle atrophy begins within a twenty-four- to forty-eight-hour period after your last workout.

The effectiveness of exercising with this type of equipment is that you can work the entire body and isolate each muscle group. You can perform multiple sets and reps per body part with the flex cords or use them in a circuit-training session. The flexibility feature of the cords allows you to create resistance so you can stimulate each muscle group. Some cords wrap around a bar and other cords are simply double wrapped around your hand. Even though results are not the same as you would expect from your regular routine, this type of exercise will satisfy the need for maintaining muscle tone and preventing muscle atrophy until you return home to your gym.

My flex cord workout

While traveling, the extra time you have is always a factor to consider in finding time for a workout. Here are a couple of exercise approaches for the dedicated who want to maintain their fitness and muscle-toning condition while traveling.

When I am stuck without a fitness room or local gym facility, I use my Rock-n-Roller Total Fitness System that comes with a workout video I produced for these occasions. A typical workout in my room with the Rock-n-Roller flex cord is a simple, but challenging, fifteen-minute total body circuit-training session.

My program is designed to complete a ten-exercise circuit, performing each exercise for thirty seconds, resting for fifteen to thirty seconds, and then moving on to the next exercise until I have completed the ten-exercise circuit. You can repeat that same circuit three times for greater benefit. It is fast, high in intensity, and will stimulate your cardiovascular system.

Though circuit-training sessions take only fifteen to thirty minutes, let me suggest that you have an oxygen tank nearby. The program is an intense total body workout program. It allows you to perform the following exercises:

- Chest press (pectorals)
- Shoulder press (shoulders)
- Back rows (back)
- Abdominal crunches (stomach)
- Standing biceps curls (biceps)
- Triceps extensions (triceps)
- Dead lifts (lower back and buttocks)
- Upright rowing (shoulders)
- Inner/outer thighs and lunges (hips, thighs, and buttocks)

If time is on your side and you have the stamina needed, try doing multiple sets and reps for each muscle group. This will give you more of a muscle-building workout that actually pumps the muscles more than you can imagine. You may want to use my Rock-n-Roller Total Fitness System at home as your main piece of fitness equipment. It is very durable, effective, and inexpensive. (To order Dr. Joe's Rock-n-Roller Total Fitness System, visit my Web site at www.bodyredesigning.com.)

Traveling shouldn't have to disrupt your training or progress; you just have to be versatile and creative. Whether you are advanced or at the beginner level; there is hope for staying in shape while traveling.

SUMMARY

As you have perused these exercise floor plans, I hope you have located the plans you need and desire and that they will provide you the most help for building your body for victory. Perhaps you now have a better understanding of the problems of your particular body type and can begin to train to build better symmetry and strength. Perhaps you were in need of simple, inexpensive options to move forward with your fitness training. Maybe you are interested in specialized training, especially for the "king" muscle group, your legs. You may be a constant traveler looking for ways to keep from interrupting your fitness regimen. I trust you will be able to utilize some or all of these plans as your fitness needs change from time to time.

The most important thing to remember about exercise floor plans is to use them continually, adapting them for your changing lifestyle and age, but never abandoning them. You will never enjoy the optimum beauty and health of your body, God's "temple," without effectively developing your personal exercise regimen. Let your friends and family help you to get motivated to exercise and to stay motivated for life! In fact, include them—they can make wonderful training partners!

SECTION THREE

Builders in Action

A Twelve-Month Protocol

CHAPTER 10
Blueprints for Building a Body for Victory

After reading the preceding chapters, you have had the opportunity to review various plans that I have designed for nourishing your body, soul, and spirit—God's temple. It will be up to you to decide which plan or plans work best for you (and your family). However, even with these carefully formulated plans and ideal strategies for building a healthy body, as with building homes, there are times when not everything goes according to plan.

Another tool that builders use, especially to help prevent the unforeseen from hindering the overall building plan, is a detailed set of blueprints. This written plan gives you a detailed map of your goals, which you can refer to on a day-to-day basis, if needed. This section is designed to become that tool for you to use, guiding you through an entire year to make sure you are continually progressing toward your fitness goals.

These blueprints should help you stay the course, be focused, and know what things need to be done in certain timelines. If you dare to take the challenge of this twelve-month building plan, making these guidelines part of your lifestyle, it won't be long before you will have the pleasure of sporting a brand-new body, one that is built for victory.

BOOK IT

In addition to these blueprints, which will soon become a part of your daily lifestyle, I suggest that you keep a journal for the entire course of the year, not just to log the exercises you are choosing, along with dietary decisions, but to include spiritual experiences as well.

For example, write the scriptures you are reading that inspire you, the encouragement of a friend, or your personal prayer that articulates your goals. Reviewing this journal along the way will be a source of strength to you on a day when you may be particularly discouraged with your progress. By the end of the year, you will have recorded the experiences that helped you succeed in reaching your goals of building a body for victory. You can refer to them for your own encouragement as well as using them to encourage others.

THE IMPORTANCE OF PACING YOURSELF

As you advance toward your fitness lifestyle goals during the next twelve months, you can refer to the following two-month modules, advancing through all six modules to complete the first year. Each module includes guidelines for:

- Body/mind connection
- Diet/nutrition connection
- Exercise connection
- Your God connection

These are intended simply as guidelines to help keep you focused and challenged. You will need to refer to specific information in the earlier chapters for complete directions and information for each phase of the building project: cleansing, diet, supplementation, preparation for exercise, and exercise programs. However, this information in each two-month module will help you to map your progress as it should be happening from month to month. I have included in the exercise connection a logical progression that will be effective if followed as I have prescribed.

It is important to remember that since you are an individual, different from all others, you must take into consideration personal limitations, such as previous injuries, surgeries, your work schedule, exercise background, and eating habits. So listen to your body and pace yourself accordingly. You have the rest of your life to be healthy and fit. So approach your building plan one day at a time, and lay a good foundation for a healthy lifestyle, one that you can build upon for the rest of your life. If that is too great a challenge, I encourage you to hire a personal trainer to help you get started.

To balance the healthy development of your physical life, remember it will be necessary to address spiritual issues as well. For that reason, I have included words of encouragement for your God connection for each two-month module. It is imperative that you schedule time to cultivate a devotional life of prayer and reading the Holy Scriptures. In this way, through strengthening your relationship with God, your attitude will remain positive, your thoughts will be clearer, your soul will be filled with peace, and you will be empowered to stay focused on your goals. Ultimately, as you commit yourself to building a body for victory, you will walk in personal destiny, which will involve finding your God-ordained way to serve your fellowman.

FOR BEGINNERS ONLY:
FIRST TWENTY-ONE DAYS

For those who have not participated in a fitness program before, I suggest that you begin with this simple, twenty-one-day break-in plan for making gradual dietary and exercise changes. I have emphasized throughout the book that you start off easy. The goal is to finish the race, not just get off to a great start. So, take advantage of this twenty-one-day break-in plan. If you are experienced in exercise and accustomed to a healthy eating lifestyle, you may want to forgo this twenty-one-day plan for beginners.

Eating plan

For twenty-one days, follow my eating suggestions by making food selections that are compatible to your blood type. Simply do your best to avoid the "avoid foods" list for your blood type for the first twenty-one days. Make your food selections from the "beneficial" and "neutral" categories only. You will find these complete lists in my book *Bloodtypes, Bodytypes and You.*[1] This plan will help to orient you to the foods that will build health for you and make you aware of foods that are detrimental as well.

Exercise plan

As far as exercise goes, simply start with a daily progressive walking program. Begin your first day with between five and fifteen minutes of walking. If that is too easy, then go for thirty minutes. But listen to your body, and don't overdo it. Remember, you are building for the rest of your life. During this twenty-one days, as you are able, add more minutes to your daily walks until you reach the goal of walking sixty minutes daily. When you reach this goal, you should be ready to move on to the following twelve-month blueprint, beginning slowly with the first two-month module.

BLUEPRINTS FOR SUCCESS

Anytime of the year is a great time to make some healthy lifestyle changes. You don't have to wait until New Year's, as is often the case, in order to begin. The time to start is right now! However, I have warned you about not being impulsive and trying to get into shape in one workout. The following blueprints will help you to succeed in your long-term goals, showing you how to pace yourself and what kind of progress to expect as you do.

MODULE ONE:
MONTHS ONE AND TWO

Instead of going on a suicide mission and burning out without ever crossing the finish line, here's a fresh new approach toward long-term health by making your health and fitness program a one-year journey. The idea is to gradually progress, month by month, for long-term results instead of taking a quantum leap into failure. Now let's get into your program.

Body/mind connection

Every born-again Christian must acknowledge that his or her body is not his or her own. According to the Scriptures it was bought and paid for with the precious blood of Jesus Christ. Since your body belongs to Christ, it has become the temple of the Holy Spirit of God (1 Cor. 6:19–20). It follows, then, that you must think of taking care of your body as an obligation to God, not an option for yourself. When you accept this truth, your motivation to develop a healthy body will become a godly desire to be a faithful steward of your body, God's temple.

By embracing this biblical truth, you will begin to be extremely cautious about what you do with your body. Your heart should be to honor God in your body and soul. With this in mind, you will want to avoid physically abusing your body with alcohol, drugs, cigarette smoke, and overeating. You won't neglect your body and threaten your health through poor eating habits and being physically inactive. On the other hand, you will not become obsessed with your physique, because your body will then be the focus point of life, which would become idolatry.

> *You must think of taking care of your body as an obligation to God, not an option for yourself.*

My strategy for helping you get in shape, designed for the entire year, is progressive in nature. As you follow it step by step, you will see how physical fitness and spiritual fitness become easily adaptable into your lifestyle. I want you to gradually become aware of how important you are to God, of your identity in Christ, and the wonder that your body is His temple—a place where His divine presence dwells. By honoring Christ as a faithful steward with your physical body, you will overcome destructive patterns touted by our society, and you will become a walking testimony of stewardship and the divine presence of Christ.

Diet/nutrition connection

It is very important to eat regularly, so try not to skip meals. Ideally you will want to eat three meals with two in-between-meal snacks or six meals a day. Follow the blood-type diet for maximum results. Snacks can be a handful of walnuts or almonds with an apple or peach, or a protein shake and/or bar.

It is vitally important that you drink water daily. Drink up to half your body weight (in ounces) daily. My preference, as I discussed, is alkaline water. Gradually work up to one 8-ounce glass every waking hour or until you reach your ideal amount.

Dietary supplementation is extremely important as a protection policy for a healthier body. During these first two months, start taking a multivitamin mineral supplement.

Exercise connection

For the first two months of your twelve-month program, I recommend that you follow the guidelines listed below for exercise, especially as they will strengthen your cardiovascular system.

Cardiovascular training

This type of training requires more duration (time) with low intensity (workload) and uses oxygen for fuel. This method of training is excellent for improving blood circulation, cardiac strength, fat burning, endurance, and VO2 max (oxygen) uptake. When choosing a cardiovascular exercise and/or piece of equipment, make your selection based on what you enjoy doing. This will ensure that you do not drop out of the program without reaching the success you desire.

Equipment/activity

Stationary biking or outdoor cycling, treadmill walking or jogging, outdoor walking or jogging, swimming, or any cardiovascular exercise machine.

Routine

Choose any cardiovascular exercise listed above. Begin with fifteen minutes, three times a week for the first month. This approach will help you gradually adjust to daily exercising without the concern for overload and injury. Add five minutes to your workout every other week. Perform this workout during this first two-month module.

Additional activities may include playing basketball, bowling, playing tennis, volleyball, or other team sports.

Target area: abdominal

During this first module, we will begin with the most difficult area to master: the jelly belly and love handles. They have to go. Developing strong stomach muscles will flatten and define the appearance of the stomach muscles. Strong abdominal muscles help support the lower back and reduce back injury and pain. Do the following exercises to begin your program:

- AB crunches: Lie on the floor with your lower legs on a chair, couch, or bench. Fold your arms at the chest and curl your upper torso upward until your elbows touch your thigh muscles. Return to the starting position and repeat. Keep your chin tucked at your chest. Perform three sets of fifteen reps of crunches three days per week.

Your God connection

To be more spiritually fit, you need to set aside some time each day to meditate on God and talk to Him in prayer. Make it a daily habit to get alone and be quiet, listening to hear what He wants to speak to your heart as well. As you cultivate your relationship with Him—reading the Bible, talking to Him, and expecting Him to respond as well—you will enjoy new tranquility and a sense of purpose that will begin to unfold your destiny for life. Don't be afraid to ask the questions you have about life, and then expect to see the answer in the pages of the Word of God or whispered into the depths of your heart.

MODULE TWO:
MONTHS THREE AND FOUR

Now that you have completed two months of your new fitness program, you are no doubt experiencing much of what I discussed in the beginning of this book regarding the importance of attitude in making you successful. It was your positive mental attitude that got you off the couch in the first place, and it will take a positive mental attitude to keep you off the couch for life. Staying in shape should be a lifetime endeavor, not a quick fix. So just as you are challenging your body, your attitude will need to be constantly challenged as well. Someone has said that one of the greatest discoveries of any generation is that a human being can alter their life by altering their attitude.

Body/mind connection

By now your body has made the adjustments to a more physical lifestyle, and I am sure your muscles are responding to the constant stimulation of regular exercise. You are probably experiencing more energy, stamina, muscle tone, and strength since you started, which is great. You may also have determined which diet works best for you. But unless you continually challenge your attitude, along with your muscles, you will hit a plateau. Ironically, as you become more physically fit you also become more mentally fit.

This body/mind connection is simply a reality. Your success for reaching your genetic potential will come from the strength of your mental attitude working in concert with your daily physical workouts. To avoid hitting a plateau in your progress, keep a positive attitude.

> *To avoid hitting a plateau in your progress, keep a positive attitude.*

It's amazing that our spiritual life runs a similar parallel with the physical. After we learn about the Lord's unconditional love and accept Him by faith as our Savior, our outlook on life changes. We perceive life differently, and our values change along with our priorities. However, if we are not careful to maintain and cultivate an intimate relationship with our Lord, our spiritual "fitness" will plateau similarly to our physical fitness if we neglect it. To help avoid this spiritual decline, always remember that your motivation for everything you do in life is to honor the Lord as His temple, as a home for His presence. This heart attitude will win every battle you face in any area of life.

Diet/nutrition connection

To lose that extra body fat around your waist, as well as everywhere else, avoid eating carbohydrates after 4:00 p.m.

Your last meal should be consumed approximately two or three hours before going to bed. Include protein at each meal and with each snack to help achieve muscle repair along with its fat-burning effect.

Drink one 8-ounce glass of water every waking hour or until you consume half your body weight in ounces. Sip water before, during, and after your workouts. Take a multiple vitamin, and add a fat-metabolizing supplement (if weight loss is your goal) to your daily routine for added nutritional support.

Exercise connection

Your first two months should have been a break-in period for physical exercise. Keep in mind that it is important that you continually challenge yourself. If you do not challenge your body, your progress will plateau, as we have discussed. If you remain indefinitely in the plateau, you will eventually begin to regress. That is not a good place to be; you want to progress!

Your cardiovascular workouts during these two months should generally be longer in duration and lower in intensity. To ensure you are training in a safe training zone, take your heart rate every five to ten minutes by taking a pulse reading. (Follow the target heart rate charts listed on the training equipment.) A rule of thumb for determining a safe pace is your ability to carry on a conversation without panting. As long as you can maintain that pace, you can adjust the speed and resistance accordingly.

Strength training

Your strength training should be more intensive and of less duration. The concept behind this method of training is strictly for muscle development. The greater the muscle-mass or lean-weight the better your overall conditioning becomes. Your body will benefit from improved heart strength and function, greater caloric expenditure, overall strength, and improved performance in sports or just everyday tasks.

- Strength routine: Perform three sets of ten to twelve push-ups from the knees or on the toes. Vary your hand spacing for hitting different chest, shoulder, and arm muscles. Perform three sets of fifteen deep knee bends (to a chair or bench). Keep your back straight, eyes looking forward and feet shoulder width apart. Include these resistance exercises with your cardiovascular training program.

Cardiovascular routine

Perform the cardiovascular exercise(s) you favor for forty minutes per session. Do this three days a week for the third month, and add a minimum of five minutes per session in the fourth month. (If you can add more, then do so.)

Target area: abdominal muscles

These muscles usually get a generous amount of fat coverage, and it takes consistent work to see progress in this area. Keep at it, and you will reap the rewards.

- Reverse crunches: Lie on your back with your feet crossed and off the floor and your knees bent. Place your hands palms down alongside your hips. Press down with your hands while curling your knees to your chest. Lower your butt to the floor. Repeat for three sets of ten to twelve reps three days a week. Add these to your crunches.

Your God connection

Believing that faithful caretaking of your physical body is an obligation to God requires the right attitude. I challenge you in your daily prayers to commit your body to Him. Allow the effort and sacrifices you are making toward a healthier, more fit body to be for His glory. By turning away from your former attitudes and taking on a new attitude that places Him in the center of your body, soul, and spirit, you will be able to agree with what the apostle Paul declared:

> Forgetting those things which are behind, and reaching forth unto those things which are before, I press toward the mark for the prize of the high calling of God in Christ Jesus.
> —PHILIPPIANS 3:13–14

MODULE THREE:
MONTHS FIVE AND SIX

Let me congratulate you for completing the first four months of your twelve-month protocol. I am sure you finished every area of the protocol perfectly. Then again maybe you are disappointed with the results to this point because you didn't, but don't fret. The important thing is that you are still in the race; you are still working toward your goal of building a body for victory. Unlike those who have dropped out completely, you still have the hope of achieving your goal. Progress is sometimes painfully slow, but if you determine to stay mentally focused on your goal, you will overcome hurdles and difficulties and begin to know the satisfaction of your achievements.

Body/mind connection

Staying focused is the mental difference between success and failure, winning and losing in any challenge you are facing. Every golfer knows that when putting the ball, if they misjudge the "line" to the cup even by a fraction of an inch, the ball will roll to the right or the left of the cup. They must read the line correctly and then stay completely focused in order to get the ball into the cup.

Staying focused is also the mental edge you need to succeed in your physical fitness program. In my years of experience with thousands of clients, I have learned that four months is many times the limit of time they will stay with a program; after that there is a high dropout rate. So if you plan to beat the odds of dropping out, I encourage you to take a little time to reevaluate your current mental focus to help you continue. (Please see section one, "Builders' Motivation.")

The following reevaluation strategies will help you stay the course and reach your goals:

- Go back and review your original goal(s) and see if it was realistic, considering your newly acquired knowledge. If it is not, set a new one.

- Write your goal down and place it where you can see it daily as a reminder.

- Be precise. Don't write, "I want to weigh *around* 160 pounds." Write exactly 160 pounds. If your goal is not precise, you will flounder and eventually drop out.

- Make your goal a priority in life. Attach a value to it. It is your goal and should be valued. This will help keep you motivated.

- Share your goal with someone in your life who is concerned with your welfare, has a positive attitude, and to whom you can be accountable with your cherished goal.

You should also apply these reevaluation strategies to your spiritual life. As you do, they will work wonders for helping you stay focused and develop spiritual growth. Paul challenges us to "be transformed by the renewing of your mind" (Rom. 12:2). Why? I think it's quite obvious. Without reevaluating your priorities and goals you will subtly drift from the course you are on and eventually miss your goals and purposes that God has ordained for you.

Remember, from month to month I am taking you to another level of fitness potential. You have to make the time, put in the energy, and challenge yourself. Take time to mentally focus and prioritize your efforts on a regular basis. Do an inventory check to make mentally sure you are where you want to be at this point. Stay the course!

Diet/nutrition connection

"Grazing" is ideal for getting your metabolism in motion. You can create metabolic momentum by grazing, which means consuming up to five or six small meals or snacks daily. Include protein with your meals and snacks. The idea is to have a nutritious breakfast, a midmorning snack, lunch, midafternoon snack, dinner, and evening snack. Balance the meals with plenty of vegetables, meats, and/or fish (protein) plus salads for roughage. Snacks can be a mixture of nuts, raisins and dates, or fruit with some cheese.

Protein shakes or bars are very helpful for the protein your body needs. Make your food selections as closely as possible to compatibility with your blood type. Be consistent with your vitamin supplementation, and try adding a liquid trace mineral supplement to your diet. These trace minerals are extremely valuable because you can't get them from your diet, your body doesn't manufacture them, and they are essential for vitamin assimilation.

Also try a fat-burning meal-replacement snack or protein bar between meals. Remember to stay hydrated.

Exercise connection

Don't be discouraged if you have not completed the exercise routines perfectly. Continue to give exercise a priority in your life, and try different forms to see which you enjoy most.

Cardiovascular training

If the weather is warm enough, try moving your cardiovascular training outdoors. Outdoor training such as cycling, jogging, and walking are great exercises. It is great to be outdoors in the sunshine and fresh air. Also, the natural terrain can be very challenging, particularly if you live in a hilly area.

Combine a walk/jog program for the next two months. Walk for five to ten minutes for a warm-up effect. Then jog for one minute, and walk for three minutes. Repeat that sequence for a total of twenty minutes three days a week. To add variety and increase stamina, try reversing the order. Walk for one minute and jog for three minutes. As your conditioning improves, feel free to add more time to your exercise sessions. Always remember to hydrate.

Strength training

Your muscles require continued resistance, or they will cease to progress. During these two months I want you to concentrate on the chest, triceps, and front deltoids by performing bench presses with a barbell or pair of dumbbells. Select a weight that allows you to do ten to twelve reps and perform three sets. For variety, move your hand spacing to wider-than-shoulder, to shoulder width, and then narrow your hand spacing to six inches. This will allow you to hit the chest muscles from different angles and involve the triceps and deltoid muscles.

Since the legs are king, perform three sets of fifteen reps of squats to the bench. For added resistance, hold a dumbbell in each hand before you start. Keep your back flat, feet shoulder width apart, and focus on a fixed object for balance. Include these muscle-building exercises three times a week.

Target area: abdominal

Unfortunately, the first to grow is the last to go; this is true of the size of your waistline. To redesign the shape of those stomach muscles you have to set them on fire. Your abdominal muscles should be showing real progress after four months, but I want to see you do just a little more for them. Stay with the crunches and reverse crunches, and add another exercise: leg lifts.

To perform leg lifts, do the following:

- Lie flat on the floor with your hands under your butt. Bend the knees slightly and lift your feet upward until they are just *less* than vertical to your body. Return to the starting position *without resting* your heels on the floor and repeat.

Perform the three exercises (crunches, reverse crunches, and leg lifts) in a nonstop manner, doing fifteen reps per exercise for three sets. Rest and repeat until you have completed three sets of all three exercises. Do them a minimum of three days a week, working up to five days a week as soon as you can.

Your God connection

Pray daily to your heavenly Father. Allow Him to fill your life in such a powerful and awesome way that it overflows throughout your life. Ask Him to make you God-conscious of His presence in your life throughout each day so you won't lose focus of Him. Keeping focused on Him will absolutely revolutionize your attitude regarding any and every issue and challenge you face. Your plans and purposes will become alive and exciting again, and every area of your life will become super-charged. Focus on Him first, and you will discover that reaping the fruits of your labor will come in abundance. The Gospel of Matthew says it best in chapter 6, verse 33: "But seek first His kingdom and His righteousness; and all these things shall be added to you" (NAS).

MODULE FOUR:
MONTHS SEVEN AND EIGHT

At this point you should have been making some progress ever since you started either with the twenty-one-day break-in period or with module one. Hopefully you have enhanced your understanding and application of dietary and exercise principles for reaching your personal fitness goals. To keep you moving forward and avoiding some of the pitfalls that would interfere with your progress, I'm taking you to the next level, challenging you to step outside your program guidelines and start using your instincts. This does not mean for you to ignore your program, but rather to connect with your body instincts to advance your program.

For example, how many times have you completed the final set of reps but had more strength left with which to do more? If that is the case, you left a lot of progress on the table! Or how many times did your technique get sloppy just trying to finish that final set of reps because you were supposed to do what the program said? It is important to keep using correct technique for success as well as safety. If you haven't sustained an injury yet by using sloppy form, you will.

Body/mind connection

Every day your body will respond differently to exercise. That's why it is important to connect with your body instincts. I can't tell you how many times I have gone to the gym for a workout and knew immediately after completing the first warmup set that it wasn't going to be a 100 percent day. So I adjusted my workout to my strength and energy level for that day and walked away with a productive workout—and without injury.

I am suggesting this because there are many negative influences in your everyday lifestyle, and they have the potential to ruin your workouts. To avoid unnecessary injuries as well as to avoid missing your full potential for progress, you will find it essential to follow your body instincts to take you outside your program, adjusting it as necessary. Before your next workout, check out these potential negative factors that will necessitate an adjustment in your workout:

- Mental and emotional fatigue
- Lack of quality sleep and rest
- Diet: too many simple sugars, not enough protein, dehydration
- Stress levels

Learning to listen to your body will tune you to hearing the best teacher, making it possible for you to reach maximum progress within your physical potential, regardless of your program guidelines.

Diet/nutrition connection

Consider the kinds of fruits you like and the quantity of fruit you eat each day. If you are not incorporating lots of fruit into your diet, I encourage you to do so. Especially in hot weather, fruits cool you down. While I am an advocate of eating enough protein daily, it is a fact that protein causes you to perspire, while fruits keep you cool.

Protein actually creates energy for your body's metabolism, maintaining the heat of it for several hours. So on hot days, those protein meals will "turn up the heat." Fruits, however, do not raise your body core heat; instead, they flood your body with natural sugars for energy. So if you want to stay cool, try eating more fruits along with your protein.

Always make certain your food groups are compatible to your blood type. Stay hydrated at all times, working harder at it during warmer months. Load up on your vitamins, including the liquid trace minerals. You may want to consider taking calcium as well.

Exercise connection

If you began this program during January, which is when many people make good choices for lifestyle change, then you have arrived at this exercise module in the heat of summer. (If that is not the case, this information will be important for you whenever your hot months occur). Please follow these cautions for exercising during hot weather.

Cardiovascular training

If you train outside in the heat of the summer months, cardiovascular training can be a real challenge, even dangerous, if you are not careful. This is a great time to minimize your outdoor training and get involved in some summer sports or other physical activities. Cut your cardiovascular training down to two days a week, but continue with the program and exercises you have been using.

Summer weather would be an opportune time to spend a couple days per week getting involved with team sports. You can join a softball or volleyball league to keep your activity level up while being connected with other teammates. The YMCA always has basketball leagues going on, as well as co-ed flag football leagues. You also can get connected with some of the local church and family teams. Get out there and hit some golf balls or play some tennis; just be sure to stay active.

Strength training

Keep your training cycles going during summer weather. However, now would be a good time to try a little versatility. Choose one favorite muscle group and "run the rack." Here's what I mean. If you like training your arms, do a warm-up set, and then go to the dumbbell rack and begin with the lightest dumbbell (heavy enough to do no more than ten reps). Perform one set of ten reps. Then, go up the rack in 5-pound increments, repeating one set of ten reps, until you cannot go any further. Each set is performed in a continuous nonstop tempo. Run the rack for three sets. Try this approach on every other major muscle group for the next two months.

Target area: shoulders

Let's go "around the world" (better bring some ice cubes, because your shoulders will catch on fire). Take a pair of dumbbells and sit on a bench. Do these three exercise movements nonstop: side laterals, front rises, and presses, as follows:

- With your arms hanging down at your sides, raise the dumbbells laterally to shoulder height and repeat for eight repetitions.
- Then raise the dumbbells forward until they reach shoulder height and repeat for eight reps.
- Immediately raise the dumbbells to your shoulders and press overhead for eight reps.

Rest after all three movements have been completed. Try to work up to three nonstop sets per workout over the next two months.

Your God connection

Staying connected with your heavenly Father is such a powerful and awesome connection. When you depend completely on His leading, life's distractions and negative influences that would normally interfere with your physical and spiritual life quickly lose their effect. Ask God to intervene in every area of your life. Give Him His rightful place in your life, which is to become Lord of all. Commit the familiar and unfamiliar; let go of what you know, own, and desire. Rest in the fact that He loves you perfectly and is the One who brings increase and blessing for your life.

> *When you depend completely on God's leading,*
> *life's distractions and negative influences*
> *quickly lose their effect.*

Interestingly, as we referred to listening to your body to adjust instinctively your exercise program, it is the practice of listening to the Holy Spirit, who is the ultimate spiritual Teacher, who will maximize your spiritual growth as well. Too often the average Christian holds on to just the "basics" in their spiritual life, which only lead to a stagnant and ineffective Christian life. What God has purposed for your life may never become a reality if you don't learn to listen to what His Spirit is saying. You must be willing to step outside the basics of your faith and listen to and follow the leadership of the Holy Spirit to walk in the fullness of your destiny.

MODULE FIVE:
MONTHS NINE AND TEN

Your training for the past eight months has been progressive; with each workout came more intensity. This progressive strategy is intentional, aimed at compatibility with normal muscle growth cycles. Should you have started too hard, too fast, too soon, you would have burned out by now. The purpose for gradually adding more intensity or workload to the muscle is also designed to prevent atrophy. Muscle atrophy is when the muscle loses size, shape, and strength by inactivity or lack of muscle stimulation. By progressively challenging your body over time with more intensity in each successive workout, your conditioning, muscle tone, strength, and overall physique should already be far superior than what it was when you started. (It better be!)

Body/mind connection

Now it's time to rev up your training another notch, to further challenge you by increasing the intensity of your program. If you have been true to the program, you are seeing progress not only in feeling better but also in looking better to others. If your mind has been set on honoring the Lord with your body, your walk of faith is progressing as well. Your body has really become a living billboard that portrays your faithfulness to health and fitness as a steward of the gift of God. As your body becomes more attractive, others may respond to that physical appeal in positive ways that allow you to witness to them of the goodness of God, who resides within your temple. Remember, when the people who lived in Solomon's day were attracted to the beautiful temple he built for God, they also were able to meet the One who resided in that temple: God.

Diet/nutrition connection

As you are inching your way toward reaching your potential, maximizing what God has given you, keep these key elements in mind. Ideally it is best to eat what is most compatible with your blood type. Generally your body will let you know if what you have eaten is not compatible. Usually this information comes in the form of gas, digestive disorders, sleepiness, and eventually more serious signs of elevated blood sugar and cholesterol readings.

Try to ingest 1 to 1½ grams of protein per 2 pounds of body weight since you are training on a regular basis. Let your protein sources be lean meats, some dairy, and vegetables. Also, include fruit at each meal and/or snack. A serving of grains three times per week is a good idea, but always work toward balancing your carbohydrates, protein, and fats to a 40-30-30 ratio, respectively. Remember, in order to avoid gaining weight or sabotaging your success of dropping a few pounds, do not eat carbohydrates in the evening when you shut down the engines for the day. Eat carbohydrates during the day.

You should be drinking at least half your weight in water every day by now. Continue taking the multiple vitamins, liquid trace minerals, and antioxidants. Also, include HGH (human growth hormone) if you are over thirty years of age.

Exercise connection

I promised you that during this module you would be revving up your progress toward fitness. The method by which we will accomplish that is circuit training (CT). CT is about the fastest method I know for breaking sticking points or plateaus, revving the metabolism, and burning fat while stimulating the muscles. The added bonus to CT is that it takes less time, because the intensity is way up there. This method of training for the next two months should definitely take you to the next level in reaching your fitness goal. As you progress with CT, you should expect more endurance, faster recovery, and more muscle definition, as well as having more time on your hands. First, let me explain how this will impact your next phase of cardiovascular training and strength training.

Cardiovascular training

As I have mentioned, at this point in your training it is time to rev things up. I want to incorporate into your program a combination of cardiovascular training that is performed at a faster and more intensive tempo into your program than what you were doing previously. This method of cardiovascular training is designed to work in concert with resistance training, so your program will be condensed and shortened. I want to mix your cardiovascular training and resistance training into circuit training.

Strength training

To improve on developing more muscle and muscular definition, I want to advance your resistance training. For the next two months the tempo will be increased to provide a greater blood pump to the muscles, more intensity for toning and shaping, and to improve localized muscular conditioning. Your resistance training will benefit your overall conditioning with the faster tempo and combination of the cardiovascular training, strength training, and circuit training in one workout.

Circuit training

The essence of the theory of circuit training is to use a more intensive method of training that will impact your cardiovascular system and define and tone your muscles while utilizing body fat for energy. It is short and sweet and to the point. Each workout should take a maximum of thirty to thirty-five minutes.

Begin every workout with a fifteen-minute cardiovascular warmup/workout. The purpose of this warmup is to get you in your *target heart rate* (THR) zone. For warmup instructions concerning your THR, read charts found on cardiovascular machines or in aerobic rooms. Once you are in your THR zone, *immediately* start your strength training. It is important that you do not rest, or your heart rate will drop. Staying in your THR will allow the body to utilize body fat for energy.

Circuit training requires that you perform one exercise for twenty repetitions within thirty seconds. Then take a fifteen- to thirty-second break before advancing to the next exercise. Go as heavy as you can for twenty reps. Do this with eight to ten exercises to complete one circuit. Work up to three circuits per workout.

To create your circuit routine, choose one exercise for each major muscle group: chest, shoulders, back, biceps, triceps, thighs, calves, and abs. Do this three times a week. Five times a week won't cause over-training; it will get you ready to peak for physique!

Target area: thighs/buttocks

Even with all the training and physical activities you are doing you may still need to give your legs some more attention.

Remember, they are king. This program I am presenting can be used to reduce or build the thighs and buttocks muscles. Lunges are the best exercise for shaping and toning the thighs and buttocks. As a starting position, simply stand with your feet about shoulder width apart.

Take a step forward with your right foot, way out in front of you. Keeping you back erect, dip down until your left knee touches the floor. Return to the starting position and repeat. Be sure your stance is wide enough so you don't tip from side to side, and don't allow your knee on your right leg to extend out over your toes when down in the dip position. Switch to the other leg and repeat. If your goal is to increase size of thighs and buttocks, hold a pair of 25-pound dumbbells for three sets of fifteen repetitions. If you wish to reduce their size, use no weights and do four sets of twenty-five repetitions for each leg.

Your God connection

As people of faith, we have God-given responsibilities on our shoulders that can show others the way of salvation, and we are held accountable. For example, we are responsible for positive role modeling and for being pacesetters. With these leadership roles comes accountability. The challenge is to be willing to grow in our maturity in Christ by pursuing Him one-on-one.

Our prayer should be to discover what God has planned for our particular lives; knowing who we are in Him; identifying our gifts, abilities, and talents; and then moving in that confidence to be the best we are capable of being. As we have discussed, the beauty of being people of faith is that life is all about God, not us. We know that every good work we do that pleases Him is only possible because of His righteousness in us. The apostle Paul says it perfectly in Philippians 1:6: "Being confident of this very thing, that he which hath begun a good work in you will perform it until the day of Jesus Christ." Press on, people!

MODULE SIX:
MONTHS ELEVEN AND TWELVE

For these final two months of this twelve-month protocol, I want you to start thinking in terms of *refining* your physique. As your physique takes on that new look you have acquired from all that hard work and discipline, it needs some more stimulation to get it to a peak. Besides the workout I have planned for the next two months, I want you to review the resources presented in the diet area of the book and apply them meticulously to your particular situation.

Body/mind connection

Also, I want you to start visualizing your ultimate goal for the appearance of your physique; make it a tangible vision. If you can add this aspect of mental attitude to the tools you have used to get you this far, you should be able to be the best you can be by the end of this twelve-month protocol. I call it peaking out.

We have observed how your spiritual life runs a similar parallel to the physical; you must also be continually stimulating your attitude about your relationship with God and His purpose for your life. Spiritually, you can't expect progress without spending time with the One who gives you the strength and power you need to be your ultimate best. So for the next two months, try diligently to focus on fine-tuning your body, soul, and spirit and peak out!

Diet/nutrition connection

By now your diet should be well under control. But in order to peak, you need to maintain a high-protein diet for these two months. High-protein meals and snacks will help burn fat and enhance muscle repair and recovery, besides strengthening your immune system and heart. This is vitally important because of your regular training program. Keeping the protein content in any meals, snacks, or drinks higher than the content of fats and carbohydrates gives you a fat-burning benefit. As usual, avoid eating carbohydrates in the evening. Balance out your daily servings of fresh vegetables and fruits with three to four servings per day; you can't eat too many of them. Mix up different types of grains in your diet, and be certain to eat balanced meals. Desserts on occasion won't do you in, but remember, you are not a follower anymore. You are a pacesetter.

> *Keeping the protein content higher than the content of fats and carbohydrates gives you a fat-burning benefit.*

Supplements are essential for protecting your health, supporting your homeostasis by delivering the necessary nutrients your body requires and that are missing from your meals. Include multiple vitamins, HGH (if you are more than thirty years old), antioxidants, and trace minerals. Drink that water every day and, when possible, drink alkaline water with a pH above 7.0.

Exercise connection

By now, exercise is a regular part of your life, and you have left the old sedentary ways far behind. You have more knowledge and understanding, not only of the importance of exercise to your health and fitness, but of ways to implement it effectively in your life. Here are the final ways I suggest you continue with your exercise program.

Cardiovascular training

Improving your cardiovascular condition helps you understand by experience that this method of training is the greatest for developing maximum aerobic capacity. Now that you have spent nearly ten months of training, built your endurance as well as enjoying the "runner's high" by releasing endorphins, you should be ready to custom design a cardiovascular training program that suits you the best.

You are no longer the amateur; you are advanced in your understanding of cardiovascular training. My recommendation for the next two months is to implement the cardiovascular training system you like the most. Use what you have learned, and challenge yourself so you can create the perfect blend of aerobic conditioning to help minimize extra body fat. Challenge yourself so you can continue to break any potential plateau. Your training schedule should include a minimum of forty-five minutes a day for five days a week. The time has come to peak!

Strength training

There is no question that strength training is the epitome of exercise methodologies for gaining muscularity: muscle strength and development. Since you have been gradually increasing your workload by adding new exercises, sets, and reps over the past ten months, I have no doubt that your body has taken on a new look that is prime for fine-tuning. Now it is time to feel your way through each workout. Get rid of your written program, and let the mirror and your experience be the refiner's tools. Listen to your body's response and train accordingly—instinctively.

If time is a factor, then circuit train. If size is part of your goal, intensify your workout by hitting those targeted muscle groups a little harder. The poundage, types of machines, or equipment should not be a factor anymore. Just use the tools you need to peak that fine-tuned body. If a muscle group is lagging and making your physique appear out of balance, spend more time on that particular area. It's time to pull out all the stops and let it rip! Your body is ready and able to handle what you give it!

Target area: total body symmetry

At this point, you have done enough work throughout this year that your body has become symmetrical and balanced.

All you have to do is be creative, try new exercises, or stick with ones that do the most for you. Remember, your success is a result of a combination of fat burning, diet, and targeted exercises. These muscles groups can be peaked out in just a few short, intense workouts per week when done correctly. Balancing and fine-tuning your physique always requires good technique.

Your God connection

Fine-tuning your life in Christ includes all areas of your existence. It is the continued discipline of putting Christ on the throne of your heart that will produce the balance you need. As you daily surrender your total person to His control, the harmony of body, soul, and spirit takes form. Your faithful effort for being God's child will pay off in your marriage, family, work, ministry, profession, and finances as well as your physical training. Your entire life continues to be a transformation from what it once was to what it can be with the Lord Jesus at the controls. According to the Scriptures, we are complete in Him: "For in him dwelleth all the fulness of the Godhead bodily. And ye are complete in him" (Col. 2:9–10).

CHAPTER 11
Builder's Walk-Through

As you may know by now, building a house is no easy task. It takes a lot of work, which is why the building process goes in phases. Also, the construction of the house requires skilled workers who know how to do their jobs, and, of course, it takes time to complete the building project. Once the actual building project is complete, before you can take residency, the builder will contact you to do a walk-through. This is your opportunity to inspect his work and see how the house looks in its finished phase. This is the time you will go through a checklist to make certain everything meets your approval.

Throughout this book you have the various strategies or building plans to choose from in all the areas necessary to have a healthier and more physically fit body. Along with the plans are all the tools you will need to accomplish the task. We also included in your building package the spiritual aspects involved, so you should have everything you need for building a body for victory in every area of your life.

If you were building a house, I would suggest that you have a checklist you can review during each building phase as well as the final walk-through. This way you can catch potential mistakes before they occur. Using this builder's metaphor for building your body for victory, I would like for you to go through this checklist just to make sure you are prepared properly for your body redesigning job. This checklist will help you stay focused on your purpose.

☑	**CHECKLIST FOR MY FITNESS PROTOCOL**
☐	See your physician for a checkup before you begin your fitness program. Get a picture of your current health condition so you have an idea of where you are from the beginning. It may take a little of your time. But it is a smart move, especially if you are a female over thirty-five years of age or a male over forty years of age. So go ahead and get the green light to go.
☐	Be sure to have a good pair or two of walking shoes. Check out your local sporting goods stores or shoe store. If you are going to get serious about training, then a backup pair is a good idea.
☐	Wear something that is loose fitting and lightweight when you exercise. This will allow your body to stay cooler while you workout and let you move freely.
☐	Always take water with you wherever you train. It is very important to stay hydrated whether you train indoors or outdoors. Drink water before, during, and after each workout, plus throughout each day.
☐	Get a notebook, so you can keep an exercise log or journal. Mark down the date, day, and the time of every workout session. Make a notation of how you were feeling before and after each workout. Use a workout chart (from your local gym) to write down the repetitions, sets, and amounts of resistance/weights you use per workout. You will be able to go back to your training journal from time to time to double check on your progress, especially if you find yourself hitting a plateau. This journal is also a great place to write down your goals. Set short-term goals for yourself. These will keep you motivated because they will be easier to reach. Write down the exact goal, and place a future date when you would like to reach that specific goal. Use a pencil just in case you have to erase a date or two.
☐	Hire a personal trainer if you are a beginner and need someone to help you get started. A good trainer will help you avoid many of the common pitfalls, such as not performing the exercises correctly, doing too much at first, and not understanding what the different pieces of equipment are for. Ask for some references to call, ask if they are certified, and see if they have a portfolio of before and after photos of their clients for you to look at. Those pictures are worth a thousand certifications. A personal trainer will also help you stay accountable and motivated. Once you learn what you need, eventually you can venture off on your own.

☑	**CHECKLIST FOR MY FITNESS PROTOCOL**
☐	Set a regular routine for yourself, and stay with it. Your body functions best with regularity. For example, some people like to exercise in the morning. If you find exercising in the early morning is best for you, schedule morning workouts for yourself.
☐	Eat at least one hour before your workouts. A high-protein meal is not going to digest within one hour, so think in terms of complex carbohydrates and starches.
☐	Don't go all day without eating for any reason, especially if you are scheduled for an evening workout. Showing up on empty is not a good thing to do because you will hit the wall before the workout is over. Your workout will come to screeching halt, and there won't be anything anyone can do for you, except drag you off to a cool air-conditioning duct so you don't overheat.
☐	Don't eat immediately before your workout because everyone will get to see what you just ate, and that's just not right!
☐	Make your food selections compatible for your blood type. Use my 80/20 rule. Work your way up to 80 percent of your food selection compatible for your blood type, and the remaining 20 percent can be for taste alone and won't affect your progress or health. This way you have some slack and won't have to put so much pressure on yourself.
☐	Don't skip meals. If you must, then eat or drink a meal replacement.
☐	Include plenty of fresh, wholesome foods like vegetables and fruits in your diet daily.
☐	Avoid processed foods (which are nutritionally useless).
☐	Drop your sugar intake to a trace or condiment amount.
☐	Avoid drinking sodas. They are very acidic and loaded with chemicals.
☐	Take your dietary supplements daily.
☐	Eat your last meal approximately three hours before retiring for the evening.
☐	If you juice fresh vegetables and fruits, be sure to drink the mixture within fifteen minutes of preparation.
☐	Maintain positive thoughts. Look on the bright side of every event. Refuse any negativity that people say about you or others.

☑	**CHECKLIST FOR MY FITNESS PROTOCOL**
☐	Pray daily.
☐	Dedicate your workouts, diet, and lifestyle to God.
☐	Include your spouse and family members to be a part of your healthy lifestyle. It will do wonders for everyone's motivation.
☐	Stay balanced in your attitude about health and fitness. Obsession or neglect are both unhealthy attitude choices.
☐	Enjoy your life.

EPILOGUE

If there is one primary message I would like for you to hear to help motivate you, it would be that God designed your body for victory in its original design, and all you have to do is faithfully maintain it. By being a faithful caretaker of your physical body, you won't miss out on the fullness of the blessings and purpose God has placed on your body as well as the witness it should portray.

The human body is a wonder of creation and comes in all shapes, sizes, and colors. Though it is complex, resilient, and durable, in many cases it is neglected or abused, or, in the opposite extreme, it becomes an obsession and focus of worship. It is the one part of humankind's total makeup that is most visible and most often misjudged by its appearance. We have each been given just one—each uniquely individual and different from the next. Like the house in which you live, your body provides the outer framework for the person who resides on the inside while directly connecting you with the world around you. As you have learned in this book, your body is a tabernacle—God's temple.

My purpose for writing this book has been to help you get more connected with your entire being: body, soul, and spirit. The diet programs, dietary supplementation, and exercise programs I have provided are intended to serve as "floor plans" for building your physical body. They are easy to follow and very effective—and with honest effort on your part, they will contribute to your new walk in victory.

Yet as awesome as the role is that your body plays in your total being, it has its limitations if the role of your mental attitude, your soul, is excluded. It is a scientific fact that your thoughts and attitudes can interfere with your body's natural functions, thus contributing to disease. Mentally, you are responsible for believing in yourself, keeping a positive attitude, and staying focused on building a body for victory. If you do, the mental side of your total being will give you victory over the common mental and emotional struggles and defeats that are part of the journey of healthy living. It will be your thoughts and attitudes that determine your success at fulfilling your destiny.

To balance your body and soul you must also include the spiritual side of your total being. I have long been impressed with the wisdom of King Solomon, who built the temple for God. Solomon was motivated by his love for God, who, in return, told Solomon that He would fill the temple with His glory. (See 2 Chronicles 5:14.) From a spiritual perspective, the born-again believer's body is the temple of the Holy Spirit. Spiritually speaking, it is what your heart is willing to embrace that determines the outcome of your belief system.

If love motivated King Solomon, the wisest man ever, then your spiritual motivation for building a body for victory should be your love for God. Through this love, your body becomes a temple of honor.

Making the healthy lifestyle changes I have outlined in this book will take on a new perspective when you are motivated by your love for God. You will discover that there is a greater good than just reaping the many physical and mental blessings you will receive from a healthy body. As your body improves and becomes more fit and healthy, it will become a focus point for people who see those changes in your body. They will want to know what you have done, how you did it, and what motivated you. You will be able to tell them of your love for God, the One who resides within your temple.

Can you think of a better reason for building a body for victory?

APPENDIX A
World Religions and Food

The following world religions and cultures have been chosen as examples to cite specific regulations concerning food that they regard as integral to their religious practice. These are very brief summaries, limited only to certain dietary considerations, for the purpose of comparing evangelical Christianity's beliefs (or lack of them) of the importance of properly caring for our body, which the Scriptures call the "temple of God."

JEWISH DIETARY LAWS

Of course, there are currently three major divisions among Jews: the Orthodox, who observe all laws in all details; the Reformed, who do not accept the Torah's dietary laws as permanently binding; and the Conservative, who are somewhat removed from the Orthodox but not as far removed as the Reformed in regard to dietary laws.

- Kosher (*kasher*): This Hebrew word means "fit" and refers to the "fitness" of food for human consumption.

- *Kashrut*: The Hebrew word for Jewish
  dietary laws written in the Torah (the first
  five books of the Bible) that are followed
  today to maintain spiritual health—not
  physical health.

Restrictions and prohibitions

There are many classifications of dietary laws, especially
those governing the use of animal foods, including the following:

- Animals permitted and others forbidden
- Approved methods for slaughtering ani-
  mals
- The examination of animals slaughtered
- Parts of animals that are forbidden
- The preparation of the meat
- The law of meat and milk
- The products of forbidden animals
- Their examination for insects and worms

Symbolic significance of foods

There is interesting symbolism surrounding particular
foods, drawn from their significance in the Scriptures. For
example, bread is a major staple that is eaten at every meal. It
signifies dependence on God for the manna, or "bread from
heaven," that the Israelites ate for forty years as they wandered
in the wilderness.

Oil, which was especially important for nomads, symbolizes prosperity. Wine symbolizes communal joy, though
drunkenness through excess is condemned.

Vegetables most common for the Jews were probably leeks,
onions, cucumbers, garlic, herbs, and spices for the wealthy.

Foods and Jewish holidays

As with most cultures, Jews used particular foods to celebrate feasts and holidays. The following are some of the ways Jews use food to celebrate:

- Sabbath—Common foods include *challah,* a bread whose name signifies more than "the staff of life." A pinch of the dough is symbolically cast into a fire in memory of the "first portion," or the tax given to the priest in the Old Testament days. They would also include fish, chicken, beans, potatoes, and *kugel* (noodle pudding). All foods are prepared before the Sabbath begins.

- Rosh Hashannah—Foods for this important holiday include challah, as well as apples dipped in honey and special sweets. No sour or bitter foods are eaten with this celebration.

- Yom Kippur—The first day of Yom Kippur is observed by a complete fast, eating nothing. The meal eaten immediately before Yom Kippur is bland to prevent thirst during the fast. The meal eaten to break the fast includes dairy foods or fish, fruits or vegetables.

- Passover—This holiday calls for a festive meal including chicken soup, matzo balls, and meat or chicken. No leavened bread is eaten on this day.

MORMONS

This religious belief system is one of the youngest religions, having developed in the United States based on revelations given to Joseph Smith, including dietary laws of health. The Mormons' diet is based primarily on the consumption of grains, particularly wheat.

Restrictions and prohibitions

Adherents are required to fast one day a month. Other dietary restrictions or prohibitions include no use of tobacco, alcoholic beverages, coffee, or tea (no products containing caffeine), and only eating meat sparingly.

ISLAM

The Quran, the Islamic holy book, contains dietary regulations. Islamic dietary laws regard eating as a matter of worship as well as a means of survival and good health. Self-indulgence is prohibited; one should never eat more than two-thirds of their capacity.

Food is never to be thrown away, wasted, or treated with contempt. Sharing food is recommended especially with the poor. All permissible foods are referred to as *halal*; harmful foods, which are prohibited, are known as *haram*.

There is some diversity in dietary habits between local cultures. For example, the Indonesian Moslems have different strictures than the Arab Moslems.

Restrictions and prohibitions

Interestingly, food restrictions and prohibitions are very similar to Jewish dietary restrictions. They include:

- No pork, carnivorous animals, or blood
- No four-footed animals that catch prey with their mouths
- No birds of prey that seize with talons
- No improperly slaughtered animals (similar to kosher meats)
- No alcoholic beverages or intoxicating

drugs, except medicinally
- No stimulants such as coffee or tea, and no smoking tobacco

Fasting regulations

All adherents to Islam must fast throughout the month of Ramadan. During this major fast, they abstain from food, drink, smoking, and sex from dawn to dusk, eating only when it is dark.

HINDUISM

Most Hindus are vegetarians, considering meat and other foods a hindrance to the development of the body and mental abilities. While they do not consider it sinful to eat meat or drink wine, they believe greater spiritual progress can be made by abstaining from them.

Restrictions and prohibitions

The Hindus do believe that the cow is sacred and is not to be killed or eaten. Other restrictions and prohibitions include:

- No pork
- No fish with ugly heads, snake heads, snails, crabs, fowl, cranes, ducks, camels, or boars
- No alcoholic beverages
- No garlic, turnips, onions, mushrooms, or red-colored foods such as tomatoes and red lentils

BUDDHISM

Buddhism is derived from Hinduism, but it advocates midway between asceticism and self-indulgence. Buddhists believe that all persons are equal in spiritual potential. Their dietary practices are highly different, depending on culture and location.

Restrictions and prohibitions

General restrictions and prohibitions include:

- Most live as vegetarians (lacto-ovo).
- Some eat fish.
- Some abstain from beef, influenced by Hindus' sacred cow.
- Some eat meat if they did not kill the animal themselves.

APPENDIX B
Dr. Joe's Health Pack

(All of the following products are distributed by Body Genetics and are available online at www.bodyredesigning.com.)

COLON HEALTH

Body Genetics INNER OUT: Fourteen-day colon cleansing and detoxifying system

The INNER OUT Colon Cleansing and Detoxifying System is designed to generate a progressive cleansing effect on your body for fourteen days. It does this in three phases. The primary colon cleansing and detoxifying effectiveness revolves around the ingredients found in the phase two Cleansing and Detoxifying Powder. These ingredients team together with the other nutrients in the capsules to perform a proper colon cleansing and detoxifying process, which may be a great asset in the maintenance of optimum health.

Body Genetics Psyllium: Fiber in capsules

Psyllium fiber in capsule form provides an easy-to-take method for adding fiber to your diet for regularity purposes. Fiber provides the necessary bulk for speeding up the transit time for proper elimination. It helps prevent the buildup of waste and toxicity in your colon while contributing to lowering your bad cholesterol.

Body Genetics Cape Aloe: Herbal laxative

Cape Aloe is an herbal laxative formulated to aid in chronic constipation. The herbal complex is powerful and generally produces bowel movement in six to twelve hours.

Body Genetics Digestive Enzymes

This digestive enzyme matrix is loaded with a complete line of enzymes to meet any shortage of enzymes missing in your digestive system. Each capsule contains the matrix of enzymes that provide the specificity of enzymatic action for every food group allowing better digestion, assimilation, and uptake of nutrition from the foods you eat.

MULTIPLE VITAMINS/MINERALS

Body Genetics AM/PM MULTI-VITAMINS

This daily multivitamin supplement is specially formulated for blood types O, A, B, and AB. Each formula contains vitamins, minerals, antioxidants, and herbs that are specifically formulated to meet the nutritional requirements of each blood type.

Body Genetics ConcenTrace

ConcenTrace, a liquid trace mineral and one of the secrets to good health and longevity, is found in the soil! This source of organic trace minerals has a similar complement of precious organic trace minerals. We are made from dust of the earth, and this dust, our own soil, is greatly depleted. ConcenTrace liquid trace mineral supplement is a very necessary and healthy choice.

Body Genetics Coral Calcium/Mega Mineral Complex

Coral calcium is a priceless organic mineral and essential for the function of every organ and gland plus imperative for balancing the blood and tissue pH in the body. Calcium is the major mineral our body needs in abundance, yet it is the most difficult mineral to absorb. Coral Calcium marine grade, which is imported from Okinawa, Japan, contains magnesium and vitamin D_3 (cholecalciferol), and is formulated to promote proper assimilation in the body.

PROTEIN

Body Genetics Protein Shakes and ThinTastic Protein Bars

Protein is essential for your body. Your body could not function without it. You need enough protein on a daily basis. Other than food sources, you should supplement your diet with a shake or bar as an afternoon pick-me-up or midmorning grab-and-go. Whatever your preference, be certain to include enough protein throughout every day.

WATER

The Alkalizer Machine distributed by Body Genetics

This machine attaches to a sink faucet and restructures ordinary city tap water into chemical-free alkaline water. It not only filters out the chemicals that make our drinking water unhealthy, but it also retains all the alkaline minerals that are in the water: sodium, calcium, magnesium, and potassium. It also reduces the molecular size of the water by half, and through electrolysis and an electrical charge, it drives more water (alkaline not acidic) into your cells.

You can go without eating for days, even weeks, but you cannot go very long without water. Every cell in your body is craving for the quenching effect of hydration. Revitalize your cellular strength, bring more life into your skin, and supply your body with organic minerals that protect it from disease and chemical imbalance with every drink of water. Drink alkaline water.

ANTIAGING HORMONE

Body Genetics Homeopathic rHGH/HGH Release

To roll back the clock is impossible, but to slow down or reverse the negative effects associated with the aging process is possible. By replacing what time and nature can no longer produce by supplementing with rHGH, you can enjoy a better night's sleep, more energy, smoother-looking skin, lower cholesterol, lower percentage of body fat, and feelings of youthfulness. You once had enough HGH, but now be certain that you still do. This antiaging hormone is orally absorbed.

There are many other nutritional supplements I could have listed. But for our purpose of covering all the major bases, I feel these will go a long way in your pursuit for building a body for victory.

For further information on Dr. Joe's Health Pack and
Body Genetics Products, contact Dr. Joe at
Body Redesigning by Joseph Christiano
P. O. Box 951479
Lake Mary, FL 32795
Telephone: 1-800-259-2639
Web site: www.bodyredesigning.com

APPENDIX C
Meal-Replacement Snacks

THERMOBLAST CHOCOLATE
MEAL-REPLACEMENT BAR
(WITH FAT-BURNING INGREDIENTS)

Dr. Joe says, "This is a meal in itself. It's convenient, satisfying, and loaded with fat-burning ingredients."

The meal-replacement bar creates a thermoblast when it comes to losing weight. It is formulated to increase the body's ability to burn calories. Its unique proprietary blend of non-ephedrine herbs works synergistically to cause the body to use fat for energy. It comes in delicious dark chocolate and serves as the perfect meal replacement for weight-loss enhancement. It is loaded with over seventy antioxidants for cellular and cardiovascular protection.

Suggested use: Grab and go! It's easy to carry wherever you go. Eat it in place of a meal. The bar works best when taking the ThermoBlast Energy Booster/Fat Burner capsules.

Benefits: Stimulates the metabolism and enhances weight loss by causing the body to use fat for energy. It's delicious, cuts sugar cravings, and is satisfying and filling. When skipping meals, the chocolate meal-replacement bar is a perfect substitute to keep an active basal metabolic rate (BMR).

THERMOBLAST STRAWBERRY-FILLED COOKIES
(WITH FAT-BURNING INGREDIENTS)

Dr. Joe says, "When limited for time, replace any meal with a cookie and my Body Genetics Protein Shake."

The strawberry-filled cookies have been formulated to serve as a meal replacement or snack. The awesomely delicious taste makes weight loss fun, tasty, and satisfying. Each cookie is naturally prepared and has a unique proprietary blend of natural ingredients that work synergistically to stimulate the metabolism for weight loss.

Suggested use: Enjoy one cookie and a Body Genetics Protein Shake in place of one or two meals per day. Enjoy them as a midmorning or midafternoon snack. They work best when taking the ThermoBlast Energy Booster/Fat Burner capsules.

Benefits: The strawberry-filled cookie aids the metabolism for additional calorie burning, satisfies cravings for sweets, and serves as a fat-burning meal replacement or snack.

THERMOBLAST ENERGY BOOSTER/
FAT BURNER CAPSULES

Dr. Joe says, "These tablets will increase your energy, help you loose weight, and improve your physical and mental performance."

The ThermoBlast Energy Booster/Fat Burner capsules are a non-ephedrine, thermogenic supplement designed to enhance weight loss. Each tablet has a unique proprietary blend of natural ingredients that work synergistically to stimulate the metabolism for weight loss and increased energy. The tablets cause no adverse side effects commonly associated with weight loss and energy products that use ma huang and/or ephedra.

Suggested use: Take one tablet first thing in the morning and one tablet midafternoon.

Benefits: Burns calories, suppresses appetite, improves performance, and increases energy and mental alertness.

For further information on
ThermoBlast Meal-Replacement Products,
please contact
Body Redesigning by Joseph Christiano
P. O. Box 951479
Lake Mary, Florida 32795
Phone: 1-800-259-2639
Web site: www.bodyredesigning.com

APPENDIX D
Troubleshooting Your Body Genetics

THE PEAR BODY TYPE (Bottom Heavy)

PROBLEMS
PREDISPOSED GENETICS

The following are the primary inherent genetic factors:

1. Narrow shoulders due to short clavicles

2. Shallow and small bustline due to less upper body fat

3. Wide pelvic and hip structure

4. Excessive adipose fat tissue (cells) on the hips, thighs, and buttocks

5. Straight waistline due to narrow or small ribs

The Pear gains weight mostly in the hips, thighs, and buttocks.

LOWER BODY

1. Most body fat accumulates in the hips, thighs, and buttocks.

2. Considered bottom heavy

THE PEAR BODY TYPE (Bottom Heavy)

UPPER BODY

1. Generally slender
2. Shallow bustline
3. Narrow shoulders
4. Straight waist

PEAR BODY REDESIGNING STRATEGIES

UPPER BODY

Perform exercises designed to:

1. Fill out the chest/bust
2. Broaden back and add width to the shoulders
3. Firm and tone the arms (biceps and triceps)
4. Firm the abdominal muscles

LOWER BODY

1. Isolate hips, thighs, and buttocks
2. Elongate, firm, and tone
3. Reduce lower body major muscles

Note: Avoid any exercises or physical activities that would tend to stimulate the lower body to grow. Concentrate on building muscle mass for the upper body while reducing the lower body.

See www.bodyredesigning.com for the *Pear Shape Workout Video*

THE APPLE BODY TYPE (Top Heavy)

PROBLEMS
PREDISPOSED GENETICS

The following are the primary inherent genetic factors:

1. Excessive adipose tissue (cells) on the upper body, usually in the abdominal region, the chest/bust, back, and arms

2. Abdominal muscles usually protrude forward or bulge outward

3. Generally a longer upper torso and shorter lower torso

4. Thin legs and buttocks, in some instances too thin or undersized from a symmetrical viewpoint

The Apple gains weight mostly in the upper body and lacks upper body/lower body symmetry or balance.

LOWER BODY

1. Upper body stores most of its body fat around the waist, upper back, and arms.

UPPER BODY

1. Lower body generally leaner but lagging in size in compared to upper body

APPLE BODY REDESIGNING STRATEGIES

UPPER BODY

Perform exercises that:

1. Shape and tone only

2. Isolate abdominal muscles

LOWER BODY

1. Build upper and lower leg muscles

2. Build, firm, and tone buttocks

Note: Avoid exercises that tend to build the upper body. Concentrate on exercising the abdominal muscles while building the lower body for symmetry with the upper body.

See www.bodyredesigning.com for the *Apple Shape Workout Video.*

THE BANANA BODY TYPE (Thin Shape)

PREDISPOSED GENETICS
PROBLEMS

The following are the primary inherent genetic factors:

1. Musculoskeletal system is such that pelvic bone, ribs, and shoulder width are similar

2. Wide waistline due to #1 above

3. Adipose fat tissue (cells) evenly dispersed on upper and lower body

The Banana gains weight equally in the upper and lower body.

UPPER AND LOWER BODY

1. Mainly lacks curves or shapeliness

2. Tends to have a straight-line figure or physique

3. Tends to look square or stocky when gaining weight

4. Assumed to always be thin, but has a "fuller banana" cousin

BANANA BODY REDESIGNING STRATEGIES

UPPER BODY

Perform exercises that:

1. Firm, tone, and build muscles

2. Strengthen and tone the abdominal muscles

LOWER BODY

1. Elongate the thighs

2. Firm and tone the buttocks

Note: The "thin" Banana body type should perform exercises that will build muscle. Because the upper and lower torsos are relatively balanced or symmetrical, the added muscle weight will enhance the total body evenly while adding curves.

BEWARE OF BECOMING A "FULL BANANA"!

See www.bodyredesigning.com for the *Banana Shape Workout Video.*

For more detailed information on body types, please visit my Web site at www.bodyredesigning.com or refer to my book *Bloodtypes, Bodytypes and You.*

NOTES

CHAPTER 4: **Dietary Dilemma**

1. Paul Fieldouse, *Food and Nutrition* (London: Croom Helm, Ltd., 1986), 11, quoted in "Religions and Food: Religious Determinants of Food Choices," Eat-online .net, http://www.eat-online.net/english/education /religion_and_food/religious_determinants.htm (accessed October 10, 2003).

2. Ibid.

3. M. E. Lowenberg, et al., *Food and Man* (New York: John Wiley and Sons, 1968), 126, quoted in "Religions and Food: Religious Determinants of Food Choices," Eat-online.net, http://www.eat-online.net/english /education/religion_and_food/religious_determi- nants.htm (accessed October 10, 2003).

4. "Religions and Food: Religious Determinants of Food Choices," Eat-online.net, http://www.eat-online .net/english/education/religion_and_food/ religious_determinants.htm (accessed October 10, 2003).

5. Ibid.

6. Ibid.

7. Ibid.

8. Ibid.

9. L. E. Grivetti, "Food Prejudices and Taboos," *Cambridge World History of Food* (N.p.: Cambridge University Press, n.d.), quoted in SIRC: Social Research and Trends Analysis, Timeline, http://www.sirc.org

/timeline/1938A.html (accessed February 26, 2004).

CHAPTER 5: **Building Phase One: Interior Work**

1. Albert Zehr, PhD, *Healthy Steps to Maintain or Regain Natural Good Health* (Burnaby, Canada: Abundant Health Publishers, 1990), 38.
2. Ibid., 34.
3. Teresa Schumacher and Toni Schumacher Lund, *Cleansing the Body and the Colon for a Happier and Healthier You* (n.p., 1987), 15.
4. Zehr, *Healthy Steps to Maintain or Regain Natural Good Health*, 35.
5. Ibid.
6. Ibid.
7. Ibid., 38.
8. Ibid., 39.
9. Ibid., 41.
10. Ibid.
11. Schumacher and Lund, *Cleansing the Body and the Colon for a Happier and Healthier You*, 10.
12. Ibid.
13. Ibid., 26.
14. Ibid., 10.
15. Ibid., 13.
16. Ibid., 11.
17. For more information on eating for your blood type, see my book *Bloodtypes, Bodytypes and You* (Lake Mary, FL: Siloam, 2000, 2004).
18. See Appendix B, "Dr. Joe's Health Pack," for more information about my Body Genetics INNER OUT Colon Cleansing and Detoxifying System.

CHAPTER 6: **Building Phase Two: Your Food Pantry**

1. Christiano, *Bloodtypes, Bodytypes and You.*

2. Steven M. Weissberg, MD and Joseph Christiano, APPT, *The Answer is in Your Bloodtype* (Lake Mary, FL: Personal Nutrition USA, Inc., 1996).

3. Ibid.

4. Ibid.

5. See *Bloodtypes, Bodytypes and You* for a complete list of foods to avoid for your blood type.

6. Dana Q. Rothacker, Beth A. Staniszewski, and Peter K. Ellis, "Liquid Meal Replacement vs. Traditional Food: A Potential Model for Women Who Cannot Maintain Eating Habit Change," *Journal of the American Dietetic Association* (March 2001): http://www.findarticles.com/cf_dls/m0822/3_101/72764296/p1/article.jhtml.

7. Marion Flechtner-Mors, et al., "Metabolic and Weight Loss Effects of Long-Term Dietary Intervention in Obese Patients: Four-Year Results," *Obesity Research* 8, no. 5 (August 2000): http://www.obesityresearch.org/cgi/content/full/8/5/399-402.

CHAPTER 7: **Building Phase Three: Dietary Supplements**

1. Dr. Alexander F. Beddoe, *Biologic Ionization As Applied to Human Nutrition* (n.p.: Whitman Publications, 1984, 2002), 39.

2. Ibid.

CHAPTER 9: **Building Phase Five: Choosing Your Exercise Program**

1. For information about Third Day Power International, go to www.thirddaypower.com or call 407-921-3604.

CHAPTER 10: **Blueprints for Building a Body for Victory**

1. Christiano, *Bloodtypes, Bodytypes and You,* 119–166.

Take charge of your health needs

We pray that you have been blessed by the message in *My Body, God's Temple*. Here are two more outstanding health books by Joseph Christiano that we think you will enjoy.

Reach YOUR Full Fitness Potential!
Satisfy YOUR unique genetic needs. Select YOUR most beneficial foods and exercises. *Bloodtypes, Bodytypes and YOU* delivers convenient food checklists, delicious recipes and vital exercises— designed especially for your blood type and body type.
$15.99/1-59185-279-X
(Paperback)

Experience New Vitality!
Increase your energy and stamina. Enjoy an active, vibrant lifestyle as you support and improve your health—seven ways.
$19.99/0-88419-693-3
(Hardcover)